PATHWAY
TO HIS
PRESENCE

CREATION
H O U S E

PATHWAY TO HIS PRESENCE

A FORTY-DAY ODYSSEY

John & Lisa Bevere

PATHWAY TO HIS PRESENCE by John and Lisa Bevere
Published by Creation House
A part of Strang Communications Company
600 Rinehart Road
Lake Mary, Florida 32746
www.creationhouse.com

Unless otherwise noted, Scripture quotations are from the
Holy Bible, New Living Translation, copyright © 1996.
Used by permission of Tyndale House Publishers, Inc.,
Wheaton, IL 60189. All rights reserved.

Scripture quotations marked KJV are from the King James
Version of the Bible.

Scripture quotations marked NIV are from the Holy Bible,
New International Version. Copyright © 1973, 1978, 1984,
International Bible Society. Used by permission.

Scripture quotations marked NKJV are from the New King
James Version of the Bible. Copyright © 1979, 1980, 1982
by Thomas Nelson, Inc., publishers. Used by permission.

Library of Congress Cataloging-in-Publication Data:
Bevere, John.
Pathway to His presence: removing the barriers to
intimacy with the Father / by John and Lisa Bevere.
p. cm.
ISBN 0-88419-654-2
Spiritual life—Christianity. I. Bevere, Lisa. II. Title.
BV4501.2.B438 2000
2 48.4—dc21   99-058695
0 1 2 3 4 5 RRD 8 7 6 5 4 3 2 1
Printed in the United States of America

INTRODUCTION

F YOU LONG FOR A DEEPER AND MORE intimate relationship with the Lord, you are not alone. You are joined on this path by the multitude who searched long before your life took shape. Even now, you are accompanied by those who currently seek the path that leads into His holy presence.

Often we are not aware of those who journey alongside us even though their paths run parallel to ours. We may meet them at occasional pools of refreshing or during times of fellowship and encouragement. But mainly this is a path we travel alone. The day will come when we all join as one and discover that though we have traveled different paths and had different experiences, we have arrived at the same destination.

This journey toward God's presence isn't attained in a single day's travel. The enemy has riddled the path with detours and roadblocks to discourage our progress, yet our Lord will use each setback to draw us closer to His side. It is a journey of a lifetime. It is a journey that prepares us for Him.

We embark on this journey when we become hungry and desperate for more of Him. This can happen at any point in our Christian walk, whether we have been saved for many years or just for a short time. It is the time when we respond to His voice calling us to go deeper and farther in Him. It is when deep calls unto deep. His voice resonates in the deep recesses of our souls, and in the stillness of the secret place we hear His invitation to know as we are known. "It is the glory of God to conceal a matter; to search out a matter is the glory of kings" (Prov. 25:2, NIV).

We are invited on the treasure hunt of a lifetime. God has hidden Himself (Isa. 45:15), and He has invited us to search for Him along the path of wisdom. He will lead and guide us along the way by the map of His Word and the examples of those who have gone before us.

We will encounter barriers on this path toward intimacy. The purpose of this book is to enable you to look deep within and search your heart for any of the hidden and often subtle blockades we will expose in these pages. Through the combination of the Word, practical applications and prayer, the blockades will fall, and the path to His presence will become clearer and more obvious in your life. May His Spirit accompany you as you accept His invitation to His glorious presence.

In His service,
John and Lisa Bevere

GOD IN THE DRY TIMES

Pathway to His Presence

The wilderness experience is different for each person. Each person's circumstances and life events will vary. You may long for a deeper relationship with the Lord, yet struggle to find God's presence. Perhaps you feel frustrated as you search for direction from God. Maybe you've prayed, and silence was the only response.

The patriarch of one of the oldest books in the Old Testament, Job, had such an experience. His life fell apart—his wealth disappeared, his sons and daughters were suddenly killed and he was struck down with a physical illness. Yet, throughout every trial, Job remained faithful and trusted the Lord. Out of his doubt and frustration, he cried, "If only I knew where to find God, I would go to his throne and talk with him there. I would lay out my case and present my arguments. Then I would listen to his reply and understand what he says to me" (Job 23:3–5). Job knew that God was in charge of his life. Yet for a time he felt that God eluded him and heaven was silent.

You may have run up against a set of circumstances that raised many questions in your mind, causing you to want to plead your case face to face with God. These dry times are ripe opportunities for heart-to-heart discussions with the Father. It is at such times that we are most receptive to His counsel and guidance. It is then that our dry spirits long for the cool, refreshing, living water only He can give.

Every Christian passes through a wilderness experience at one time or another. It's not the time to seek His hand, but a time to seek His heart.

Seeking God's heart produces character and strength. Your time in the wilderness prepares you for the Promised Land, but when you are in the middle of the wilderness, you are often tempted to feel discouraged, especially when you lack understanding.

The wilderness experience is designed to train and prepare you for a new movement of God's Spirit in your life—provided you enter the experience with wisdom and a heart for God. Enter it with the wrong attitude or simply search for an escape route, and you will probably experience hardship, frustration and even defeat. It's critical to understand God's purpose for dry times.

The children of Israel mistakenly believed that the wilderness was God's punishment, so they constantly murmured, complained and desired what they felt they lacked. When it was time for them to leave the wilderness and conquer the Promised Land, the evil reports from the murmurers and complainers held them back. When they were given a choice between God's promises and ability or man's perceptions and inability, they chose to believe man rather than God. They were ignorant of God's nature and character. They were unable to receive their land flowing with milk and honey. So God said, "OK, it will be as you believed." They could have spent only a brief time in the wilderness—instead they spent a lifetime.

If you embrace this dry time with joy, the Lord will provide you with strength for your journey to maturity. As James wrote, "For when your faith is tested, your endurance has a chance to grow. So let it grow, for when your endurance is fully developed, you will be strong in character and ready for anything" (James 1:3–4).

During the next five days we will journey through some of these wilderness experiences.

The pathway to God's presence is a journey—one that involves change and a willingness to grow and learn. Turn the page, and take a step toward His presence. Don't allow any barriers to keep you from knowing Him intimately.

When God Is Silent

6

I go east, but he is not there. I go west, but I cannot find him. I do not see him in the north, for he is hidden. I turn to the south, but I cannot find him.

—JOB 23:8–9

So often our heart's cry matches these words from Job. You long to hear from God, but silence is your only answer. You pray—yet your prayers seem to fall flat. Your frustration grows as you recall a time when you merely whispered the Lord's name and His presence was immediately there. Now in the stillness you want to shout, "God, where are You?"

Like Job who turned every way, you seek Him, yet you cannot perceive Him or His workings in your life. Welcome to the wilderness! As your toes feel the sand of the desert, know you are not alone in the journey. You walk in good company.

You walk where Moses walked…Moses, raised in Pharaoh's court as a prince; Moses, a man with a vision from God to deliver the Israelites out of bondage and slavery. It took years for his vision to become a reality. In the meantime, for forty years, Moses cared for sheep on the backside of the desert.

You also walk alongside Joseph . . . Joseph, the highly favored son of his father; Joseph, who was given dreams of great leadership and achievement; Joseph, whose own brothers threw him into a pit, then sold him into slavery, which led to prison.

You are sitting beside Job…Job, the man whom the Bible describes as "the greatest of all the men of the east" (Job 1:3, KJV); the one whom God reported that there was no one else like him; Job, who lost everything—possessions, children, health, plus the support of his wife.

Most importantly, you journey in the wilderness in the company of Jesus, the Son of God, who, after receiving the public witness of God the Father and the Holy Spirit that He was, indeed, the Son of God, was led into the wilderness to face the forces of darkness.

The procession of wilderness travelers is long because the silence is a necessary time—a season in the life of every child of God. We long to bypass this pathway, and in fact, we search for shortcuts or detours, but there aren't any. The pathway to His presence can't be reached without passing through a season in the wilderness.

As Christians, if we understand the seasons of the Spirit, we will know what God wants to accomplish and be able to respond wisely. Conversely, if we pass through God's preparation ground without understanding, we will not know what He wants to accomplish and may act unwisely.

Consider the wisdom of the farmer. It's impossible for the farmer to harvest during planting season. If the farmer doesn't plant during the season for sowing, then he will not reap his crop at the time of harvest. It is crucial to plant at the correct time. If the farmer plants too early or too late, his crop yield will be diminished at harvest time. The seeds will not be in the proper position to receive what they need to flourish.

For us to benefit from God's care and provision, we must recognize our season of preparation. We cry out for the harvest and blessing of God, yet it may not be the right season—instead it may be a season of pruning.

Like trying to harvest in the

wrong season, God wants us to understand the pathway in our intimacy with Him through the dry times. God's purpose in the wilderness is to train us, to prepare us for an even deeper intimacy. As we understand the silence of God, we can continue on the pathway with joy and God's strength.

REMOVING BARRIERS

Our path through the wilderness is a journey to a deeper understanding of God. Press into a deeper place in God through increased time in reading God's Word.

PRAYER

Father God, why do You seem silent? I pray and read my Bible, yet I feel so distant from You. Keep me on the pathway into Your presence—even when You are silent. I long to walk in a deeper intimacy with You.

In Jesus' mighty name remove any barriers in my life that prevent me from deepening my relationship with You. I long to testify of You as Job also longed to proclaim You, but You know where my path is leading. And when You have tested me like gold in a fire, You will pronounce me innocent. (See Job 23:10.)

As I take this forty-day journey on the pathway to Your presence, give me understanding and new insight about Your nature. As I walk through a wilderness experience, open my heart to learn from the experience and from You. In Jesus' name, amen.

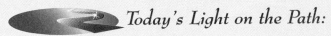 *Today's Light on the Path:*

PSALM 63 • PSALM 84

9

Why Seek Jesus?

10

*T*he next morning . . . when the crowd saw that Jesus wasn't there, nor his disciples, they got into the boats and went across to Capernaum to look for him. When they arrived and found him, they asked, "Teacher, how did you get here?"

Jesus replied, "The truth is, you want to be with me because I fed you, not because you saw the miraculous sign."

—JOHN 6:22–26

Multitudes of people came seeking Jesus. When they finally found Him, He looked at them and perceived the reason for their search. It wasn't because they had seen Jesus perform miraculous signs. They sought Jesus because they had eaten and were filled. The purpose of signs is to give directions or information. The miraculous signs Jesus performed could have pointed the people to the awesome reality that He was their Messiah. Yet Jesus knew the multitudes weren't seeking Him because of the signs and miracles; these people only wanted to fill their longing stomachs. They wanted what He could provide them more than they desired to know Him.

Too often even today we seek Jesus for the wrong reasons. Selfishly, we pursue only His benefits and blessings, rather than pursuing Him out of love and longing for Him. Without being aware of it, sometimes we use Jesus and reduce Him to a resource in a time of need.

Perhaps you've known someone who only contacts you when he needs or wants something from you. Or even worse, have you ever had a person seek your friendship, only to later discover that his motive was to gain something you have? Perhaps this person wanted your influence, money, material goods or position. In reality, this person lacked genuine concern or love for you—yet for a time you served his purpose. If you've encountered such "friends," you know how it feels to be used.

This selfish attitude has permeated our society— even in the church. Sometimes couples marry for selfish reasons. They fail to realize marriage is a covenant of love—not a contract. They marry because of what their partner can do for them. And if this partner fails to meet their expectations, they seek another partner.

Many Christians have a growing discontent, and their love has grown cold. They serve the Lord for what He can do for them—not out of love for who He is. As long as God provides their wants, they are happy and excited about Him. But when they enter a dry time, it reveals the true motives of their hearts. Any time the focus is self, complaining will begin.

Consider the children of Israel in the Old Testament. After the plagues on Egypt, they escaped. Pharaoh and his powerful military chased after the people to return them into slavery. The Lord divided the Red Sea, and the people crossed on dry land. In the process, the Lord delivered His people from the hand of Pharaoh.

The Scriptures say, "Then Miriam the prophet, Aaron's sister, took a tambourine and led all the women in rhythm and dance. And Miriam sang this song: 'I will sing to the LORD, for he has triumphed gloriously; he has thrown both horse and rider into the sea'" (Exod. 15:20–21). These people celebrated because they were overwhelmed with God's goodness and greatness. Yet only three days later, in the wilderness of Shur, they found bitter waters and began to complain against Moses and his leadership. Moses responded, "Your complaints are against the LORD, not against us" (Exod. 16:8). Their hardship only revealed their love for themselves, which kept them from the intimate knowledge of God.

In the midst of our wilderness experience, our hearts should turn away from self and turn toward seeking the Lord.

REMOVING BARRIERS

What is your own motivation for seeking Jesus? Is it simply self-serving or because you long for His intimacy? If your motivation is basically selfish, then repent of it, and turn your affections toward His heart's desires.

PRAYER

Lord, I need You every hour of every day. Fill my life with Your love, fellowship and presence. I want to seek You as a child who loves and adores You. I admit that often my motivation for seeking You has involved selfishly asking for one provision after another. Purge my heart of selfishness. Lord, You know my heart and my needs. I commit those needs and desires into Your capable hands.

Today I will turn my attitude and seek You as a loving child. Tune my heart to sing Your praise. Fill me with Your love so I can be a living testimony of Your love. Use me today to love others and to love You. In Jesus' name I pray, amen.

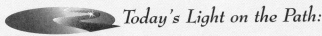 *Today's Light on the Path:*

John 5:36 • John 6

13

Turn to the Truth

*J*esus said to the people who believed in him, "You are truly my disciples if you keep obeying my teachings. And you will know the truth, and the truth will set you free."

—John 8:31–32

One step along our pathway to intimacy with God is a true and honest relationship. When you know truth, you are intimately acquainted with it. To know something is more than the mere acknowledgment of its existence. It implies a relationship. Strong's Exhaustive Concordance defines the term *know*, as found in this scripture, as "absolutely; in a great variety of applications and implications; an adherence to truth not only on a mental level, thus changing our perceptions on merely a single level, but one that permeates until it reaches every area of our being." This is what happens when truth becomes a part of us.

We need to know the truth with a deeper intimacy than we've known lies. At one time we lived under the power of lies, and they captivated us. If we live the truth, it will liberate us. To know truth is to live truth. It is the truth we live that sets us free.

Then truth penetrates deeper and reaches further than lies, dispelling with its light any darkness lurking in the remote areas of our souls. Knowledge of the truth alone will not be enough. We need a *relationship* with truth. The question changes from "*What* is truth?" to "*Who* is truth?"

I (Lisa) am married, and though others may know about my husband or know him personally on some levels, they will never know him in the same way or dimension that I do. They may be acquainted with John Bevere the friend, minister, author, employer or father. But I alone know him on the intimate, private level of husband. That is our relationship. Though others may know him by what he does, I know John Bevere by who he is. We are one.

On our pathway to intimacy with Father God, <u>we must become one with the truth because we have been one with the lie.</u> Who is the truth? Jesus answered, "I am the way, the truth, and the life. No one can come to the Father except through me" (John 14:6).

Jesus is the way we seek. He is the truth who sets us free. He is the life for which we long. You may right now be questioning what I say: "I know Him, but I do not feel free. I feel captive!" He allows captivity to serve as an invitation to experience Him on a deeper level. He is drawing you closer, drawing you deeper to His side. He wants to be your companion and Lord as you journey from captivity to freedom. He does not want you to try it again on your own strength. You've already tried and failed.

<u>Often it's easier to embrace lies than truth. One lie is easily followed by another and yet another.</u> But the lying stops when truth is discovered. <u>Truth is the only means to stop the progression of lies.</u> When we are constantly bombarded with lies, we begin to believe the lie. Likewise, when the lies occur over a long period to others and to ourselves, we begin to believe them and start doubting the truth.

God offers truth to whomever will turn to Him and seek the truth. The truth cost the very life of God's Son, Jesus. He freely calls all who have ears to hear. He wants the glory from this escape and return to intimacy. <u>All He requires from you is a deeper level of surrender to the truth, a yielding of your will to His.</u>

Pause on your wilderness journey and pray the prayer below so you can open your heart to God's truth.

REMOVING BARRIERS

Take a hard, soul-searching look at your relationship with your heavenly Father. Is it based on lies or truth? Make a commitment today to allow your mind and heart to be permeated with God's Word of truth.

PRAYER

Jesus, I have known You as Savior, Teacher and Lord. I ask You to reveal Yourself to me as the Truth. Let this light pierce through the darkness of the lie. You are the Word made flesh. As I submit to Your Word, let it become flesh to me. I embrace You and Your words as the final and ultimate authority in my life. Unveil my eyes that I might see You, and in so doing, I shall behold the Truth. In Your name, amen.

 *Today's Light on the Path:*

JOHN 8

The Impossible Task —On Our Own

18

Those who obey my commandments are the ones who love me. And because they love me, my Father will love them, and I will love them. And I will reveal myself to each one of them.

—JOHN 14:21

Jesus longs for an intimate love relationship with each of His children. Without this life-giving relationship, we can't keep the commandments. Despite our best intentions to keep the laws of God, in our own strength it's an impossible task. We struggle under the heavy weight of unfulfilled vows and promises until we are so burdened we can barely lift our voices in prayer. We feel stuck, unable to obey, so we turn to the pastor, our mates or our friends for help. We hope they will seek God on our behalf and tell us what God is saying.

I used to read John 14:21 and think the Lord said, "John, if you keep My commandments, you will prove that you love Me." I turned this verse into an additional law in my life. Then one day, the Lord told me to read this scripture again. After I read it, He said, "You did not get what I was saying—read it again." This went on until I had read the scripture ten times.

Finally I said, "Lord, forgive my ignorance. Show me what You're saying!"

He said, "John, I wasn't saying that if you keep My commandments, you will prove you love Me. I already know whether you love Me or not! I was saying that if a man falls head over heels in love with Me, then he will be enabled to keep My commandments!" God emphasizes *relationship*—not *law*. He can't be known through rules or regulations. The Holy Almighty One cannot be reduced to a formula!

Yet many people have this perception of the Lord. Instead of a relationship with God, they have substituted seven steps to healing, a four-point plan of salvation, five scriptures on prosperity and so forth. Their concept of God is wrapped up in their box of promises—promises they pull out and claim as necessary. Yet these same individuals wonder why they struggle to keep His commandments.

Have you ever fallen in love? When I was engaged to my wife, Lisa, I was head over heels in love with her. I thought about her constantly. I'd do whatever was necessary to spend as much time with her as possible. If she needed something, no matter what I was doing, I would jump in my car and get it for her. I didn't have to force myself to talk to people about her. I extolled her praises to anyone who would listen. Because of my intense love for Lisa, doing anything with her was a joy for me. I didn't do these things to prove my love. I did them because I loved her.

Just a few short years into our marriage, I turned my attention to other things, like my work in the ministry. Soon it became increasingly bothersome to do things for her. Taken for granted, Lisa wasn't the focus of my thoughts as often. My gifts for her came out of obligation on Christmas, anniversaries and birthdays, and even these times seemed like a bother. Our marriage was in trouble—our first love was dying!

God turned my heart to see my selfish actions toward Lisa. Graciously, He rekindled the flames of our love and healed our marriage.

The same thing can happen in our love relationship with God. Our love relationship with God isn't a set of rules or regulations. It's a journey of the heart. Has your first-love relationship with Jesus begun to fade? Ask God to rekindle your love relationship.

REMOVING BARRIERS

Is your relationship with God based upon a set of rules, or is it a journey of the heart? Ask God to rekindle your love relationship with the Savior. As you spend time in prayer and in the Scriptures, ask Him to replace the rules with renewed intimacy.

PRAYER

Jesus, I've fallen into a trap of trying to love You by obeying a set of rules and regulations. Instead, I want to rekindle my love relationship with You— not to have a set of dos and don'ts in my mind. Remove those "rules" about You, and help me to learn from You. You said, "Take my yoke upon you. Let me teach you, because I am humble and gentle, and you will find rest for your souls. For my yoke fits perfectly, and the burden I give you is light" (Matt. 11:29). Thank You that You can teach us to rest in You. I praise You that Your burden is light and fits perfectly.

I love You, Lord. Help me to deepen my relationship with You, and show me the pathway to Your presence. Amen.

 *Today's Light on the Path:*

JOHN 14

The Road Few Travel

22

"My thoughts are completely different from yours," says the LORD. *"And my ways are far beyond anything you could imagine. For just as the heavens are higher than the earth, so are my ways higher than your ways and my thoughts higher than your thoughts."*

—Isaiah 55:8–9

ew people have walked this road, yet now God is preparing many to begin the journey. The pathway to His presence will lead us through the wilderness, along the highway of the Lord called Holiness.

According to one definition, *holiness* is "the state of being pure." Jesus said, "God blesses those whose hearts are pure, for they will see God" (Matt. 5:8).

On some unexpected day, Jesus is coming for a church without spot, wrinkle or any such thing. (See Ephesians 5:27.) Many of us have tried to obtain holiness by obeying rules and regulations, and we've failed miserably. Like the Jews who tried (and failed) to keep the Law in order to receive salvation, we cannot walk in holiness through a series of rules and regulations. Many people have built these self-imposed restrictions with legalistic rulings on tangible things (i.e., no makeup, adhere to a strict dress code, no television). All these outward limits were established in an attempt to obtain inward purity.

God is not looking for an outward form of holiness, void of inward transformation. He wants an inward change of your heart, for a pure heart will produce pure conduct. Jesus said, "First wash the inside of the cup, and then the outside will become clean, too" (Matt. 23:26).

If your heart is pure, you will not want to dress in a seductive manner. Nevertheless, even with a dress down to the ankles, a woman can still have a seductive attitude. A man can boast that he has never been divorced, yet is he holy when he lusts in his heart for other women? No.

If your heart is pure, a television in your home will not cause you to watch or desire any impure programs. Some people try to say that if Christians have televisions in their homes, they are worldly. Electronics in your home is not a criterion for worldliness—your heart makes this determination. You can have no televisions in your home and lust after one in your heart. If your heart is pure, you will desire only what God desires.

In the wilderness, or during these dry periods in our relationship with the Lord, God purifies our motives and intentions. As you walk in the way of holiness toward an intimate relationship with God, recall again the words of Isaiah 35:8: "And a main road will go through that once deserted land. It will be named the Highway of Holiness. Evil-hearted people will never travel on it. It will be only for those who walk in God's ways; fools will never walk there." Notice that evil-hearted people never travel this highway. Those bent on evil have no interest in

purity and in following God's ways. As followers of Jesus, we want to walk on the Highway of Holiness. As we follow God's ways, we find the path toward intimacy.

REMOVING BARRIERS

Holiness is not a series of rules for conduct—but an attitude of the heart. As you come before a holy God, what changes will you make to purify your heart? Take a soul-searching look at your own motives, intentions and behaviors and make a commitment to make one heart attitude change—however small— that will deepen your relationship with Jesus.

PRAYER

Lord, the intangible results of my faith are so difficult. It's often easier to create rules and regulations about my outward behavior. Give me spiritual eyes and insight to remove these dos and don'ts from my life. Work on my heart. Remove my heart of stone, and give me a heart of flesh.

Father, I long to be pure before You and to travel the Highway of Holiness. Teach me Your ways, and help me to walk in Your path. Mold me, shape me and guide my thoughts so they constantly turn to You. Thank You that Your ways are higher than my ways and Your thoughts higher than my thoughts. Give me Your insight, and help me throughout this today and my years in the future. I love You, Jesus. By faith, I expect You to do exceedingly abundantly above all I can ask or think. Amen.

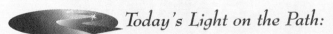 **Today's Light on the Path:**

LEVITICUS 10:1–3 • LEVITICUS 19:2 • 2 CORINTHIANS 6:14–7:1 • 1 THESSALONIANS. 4:1–8 • 1 PETER 1:13–19

Section *Two*

OBEY WHOM?

Pathway to His Presence

Obedience. The word is often whispered in disdain as our rebellious attitudes question, "Obey whom?"

Our culture prides itself on independent thinking. To say you are obedient sounds as if you are a simple-minded Christian, one who follows the Lord blindly—without forethought or understanding. Yet nothing is further from the truth. It is not the weak who walk in obedience, but the strong. The pathway to God's presence involves listening to God's voice, then obeying His revealed truth.

Abraham is called the father of all who believe. (See Romans 4:16.) God says through Isaiah, "Look to Abraham your father, and to Sarah who bore you; for I called him alone, and blessed him and increased him" (Isa. 51:2, NKJV). God didn't call a group of people—He called Abraham only. And Abraham had the courage to obey and follow God's voice. It takes courage and a willing heart to leave the comfortable, the secure and the familiar to allow the Spirit of God to lead us. Abraham left behind family, friends and the inheritance of man to fulfill God's calling. In order to know God, he came apart and followed God to an unknown land of God's choosing.

God blessed Abraham's obedience, increasing his possessions and family in the process. However, when Abraham left his comfortable surroundings and arrived at the land to which the Lord led him, he was met with a severe famine. Now stop and think about it. God promises to bless Abram (his original name), to make him a great nation and to make his name great. In obedience, Abram leaves everything and follows the Lord to a land—of famine?

28

Most of us in Abram's circumstances would have decided we had missed hearing God and returned to our homeland. Yet Abram did not let these circumstances affect his faith in God. He knew God was capable of providing during famine. Along the pathway to God, we must obey His Word and, in faith, move steadfastly ahead in our journey. Through this obedience, God reveals Himself to us in a new way.

Consider a few key people from the Bible and how they stepped out in faith and obedience:

The prophet Samuel testified David would be a king—yet David spent years in wilderness caves before he took his throne.

Joseph dreamed of a great future—then spent twelve years of hardship, first in a pit, then in slavery and a dungeon before the dream became a reality.

John the Baptist was called to be the great prophet. His father told him about the vision of his calling. The memory of that vision transported him on as he wandered the deserts of Judea for several years.

Along the pathway to His presence, God reveals Himself to us in a fresh, new way. In a prophetic song of praise, Isaiah declared, "But for those who are righteous, the path is not steep and rough. You are a God of justice, and you smooth out the road ahead of them. LORD, we love to obey your laws; our heart's desire is to glorify your name. All night long I search for you; earnestly I seek for God. For only when you come to judge the earth will people turn from wickedness and do what is right" (Isa. 26:7–9).

We continue on our pathway to His presence,

longing to know God better and to do what is right. God wanted to reveal Himself to the children of Israel, just as He had revealed Himself to Moses. But the children of Israel backed off from such an experience, saying to Moses, "You go and speak to the Lord and come to us and tell us all that He says and we will do it." (See Deuteronomy 5:27.) They never *knew* Him; they only knew *about* Him. Therefore, they never could keep His commandments, and they never entered His Promised Land. God wants us to draw near to His presence by way of obedience. Set your heart to seek God. Cleanse your hands, and purify your heart. Then move ahead in faith. Over the next five days we will examine obedience. Let's turn the page and continue our journey along the pathway to His presence.

Listen and Obey God

32

And the LORD said to Moses, "You and Aaron must take the staff and assemble the entire community. As the people watch, command the rock over there to pour out its water. You will get enough water from the rock to satisfy all the people and their livestock."...Then Moses raised his hand and struck the rock twice with the staff, and water gushed out.

—NUMBERS 20:7–8, 11

Amazingly the Lord gave the water even though Moses disobeyed God's instructions concerning how to call it forth. The water was for the people in response to their need. So God did not hold back the miracle from the people in order to punish Moses.

When Moses disobeyed and hit the rock instead of speaking to it, through his action Moses shifted the focus from God to himself. Frustrated with the people of Israel...frustrated with God because the water didn't come out immediately, Moses struck the rock as he had done previously in the wilderness of Sin. (See Exodus 17:1–7.) Perhaps Moses had become comfortable with his ability to lead, and maybe now he felt God would honor whatever he deemed best. Since Moses had not honored God before the Israelites, God prevented him from leading the people into the Promised Land.

Once again Moses had done something his own way (when he was forty he tried to deliver the people his own way), but this time the consequences were considerably greater. Moses had walked in the power and might of God, and all of his strength was derived from his dependency on God. Because Moses acted independently of God in front of the people, his action brought judgment and punishment. God said that because of this act, Moses would not lead the children of Israel into the Promised Land.

Like the people of Israel, we are on a journey along the pathway to God's presence. Our journey prepares us to walk in power and the glory of the Lord—without the sin and resulting judgment of

33

disobedience. On this pathway our pride is brought low and humility is exalted. The truly humble man walks as Jesus walked, crying, "I will not do anything until I see the Spirit of the Lord do it. In my own strength and ability I am nothing."

The prophet Habakkuk wrote, "I will climb up into my watchtower now and wait to see what the LORD will say to me and how he will answer my complaint. Then the LORD said to me, 'Write my answer in large, clear letters on a tablet, so that a runner can read it and tell everyone else. But these things I plan won't happen right away. Slowly, steadily, surely, the time approaches when the vision will be fulfilled. If it seems slow, wait patiently, for it will surely take place. It will not be delayed'" (Hab. 2:1–3).

Habakkuk declared that he would write what he saw and run with what he saw at the appropriate time. He went on to say, "Look at the proud! They trust in themselves, and their lives are crooked; but the righteous will live by their faith" (v. 4). The prophet understood that a proud soul is crooked (this is an individual who does not wait on the word of the Lord, but runs in his own strength).

So often we want to rush ahead instead of waiting on God. Receiving an answer can require patience and steadfast obedience to God's voice. As we tune our hearts in obedience to God's voice, He will show us how He wants us to live. Anything accomplished apart from His leading and ability is an exercise in futility.

REMOVING BARRIERS

Take a moment to consider your own actions. Whose power are you using, your own or God's? What active steps can you take to be more dependent on God?

PRAYER

Heavenly Father, I want to move each day in the power and might of Your Spirit. Forgive me for the times when I have disobeyed You and plowed ahead in my own strength. Give me a heart that longs for You. As I spend time in prayer listening to Your voice, speak to my heart and direct my steps.

Like the great King David, I long to be a person who has a heart after Your own. You called Abraham a friend of God. Teach me how to live in obedience to You, and deepen my relationship with You. In Jesus' name, amen.

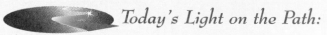 *Today's Light on the Path:*

EXODUS 17:1–7 • NUMBERS 20:1–13 • JAMES 1:22–24

Willing to Obey God's Word

36

My hands have made both heaven and earth, and they are mine. I, the LORD, have spoken! I will bless those who have humble and contrite hearts, who tremble at my word. But those who choose their own ways, delighting in their sins, are cursed.

—ISAIAH 66:2–3

How do you fear God, and how do you respond to His authority? The Bible says that someone who fears God trembles at His Word and in His presence. (See Isaiah 66:2; Jeremiah 5:22.) The idea can be summarized in one statement: To fear God is to obey Him willingly, even when it appears more advantageous to compromise or not obey His Word.

Our hearts must be firmly established in the fact that God is good. A person who fears God knows this fact because he knows God's character. That is why he or she will draw near to God even when others might draw back in terror.

The hardships that Israel faced exposed what was in the people's hearts. The children of Israel obeyed God's Word as long as they experienced immediate benefits for themselves. But the moment they suffered or could no longer see the benefits, they lost sight of God and complained bitterly.

For centuries Israel had prayed and cried for deliverance from their Egyptian oppressors. God heard them and sent their deliverer, Moses. The Lord told Moses, "I have come to rescue them from the Egyptians and lead them out of Egypt into their own good and spacious land. It is a land flowing with milk and honey" (Exod. 3:8).

Moses proclaimed God's words to Pharaoh, saying, "Let My people go." But Pharaoh responded by increasing their hardships. No longer would straw be provided for the production of their already overwhelming tally of bricks. The Israelites would have to glean by night and labor by day. The total number of bricks demanded of them was not diminished though their supply of straw had been removed. God's word of freedom had only increased their suffering. They complained under the weight of this oppression and told Moses, "Leave us alone and quit preaching to Pharaoh. You are making life worse for us."

When God finally did deliver them from Egypt, Pharaoh's heart was hardened again, and he pursued the Israelites into the wilderness with his finest chariots and warriors. When the Hebrews found themselves with the Egyptians in hot pursuit against them and their backs to the Red Sea, they complained again. "Didn't we tell you to leave us alone while we were still in Egypt? Our Egyptian slavery was far better than dying out here in the wilderness!" (Exod. 14:12).

In essence, they were saying, "Why should we obey God when it is only making our lives more miserable? We are worse off—not better." They were quick to compare their former lifestyle with their present condition. They desired comfort over obedience to God's will. Oh, how they lacked the fear of God! They did not tremble at His word.

God split the sea, and the children of Israel crossed on dry land and saw their oppressors buried. They celebrated God's goodness and danced and praised before Him. They were certain they would never doubt His goodness again! But they did not know their own hearts. Another test would arise that would once again expose their unfaithfulness. Just three days later they would again complain against God because they did not want bitter water, but sweet. (See Exodus 15:22–25.)

How often do we do the same? We want soft and pleasant words when the bitter is what's necessary for cleansing us from impurities. We need to stand firm in our obedience to God and His Word—even when it doesn't seem the natural or pleasant path.

REMOVING BARRIERS

Do you ever complain, "It would be better for me if _____"? Think carefully about each distasteful circumstance in your life. With a humble and contrite spirit, thank God for each one. Stand firm in your obedience to God—it leads to the milk and honey of God's blessings.

PRAYER

Lord, I choose to be someone who trembles at Your Word and who obeys You constantly. As I consider my actions, I realize I've longed to return to days when life was less complicated. I've acted like the children of Israel by thinking about Egypt and longing to return to a false memory.

Thank You for my past. Use those lifetime lessons to draw me closer to You today and throughout my days ahead. Teach me to follow You and thereby grow in intimacy with You. If I fall, pick me up and carry me along the pathway of intimacy and obedience. In the all-powerful name of Jesus, amen.

 *Today's Light on the Path:*

NUMBERS 13–14

Don't Just Listen—Obey

40

But be doers of the word, and not hearers only, deceiving yourselves. For if anyone is a hearer of the word and not a doer, he is like a man observing his natural face in a mirror; for he observes himself, goes away, and immediately forgets what kind of man he was.

—James 1:22–24, NKJV

When we hear God's Word and do not do it, we deceive our own hearts! A deceived person really believes he or she is obeying God, when in reality this individual is acting in disobedience. Deception veils the heart and obstructs the truth. The more a person disobeys, the thicker and more obstructive the veil becomes, making it harder to remove.

In God's eyes, partial or selective obedience is the same as rebellion to His authority. It is the evidence of a lack of the fear of God!

Once I (John) was in Canada preparing to minister. We were in the middle of praise and worship when the Spirit of the Lord posed this question: "Do you know what a religious spirit is?"

I have learned that anytime God asks a question, He is not looking for information. Although I have written and preached on religious spirits and how they operate, I knew right away that my information must have been limited at best. So I answered, "No, Lord—please tell me."

He quickly responded, "A person with a religious spirit is one who uses My Word to execute his own will!" In other words, it is when we take what the Lord has said and work our own desires into it, rather than obeying with God's desires at heart.

I stood in awe of the wisdom imparted by the Spirit of God. I applied this to Saul's situation in 1 Samuel 15:1–24. I could see how Saul had done what he was told, yet worked his own desires into his disobedience. God's heart was not his focus. Saul had seen an opportunity to benefit himself and strengthen his position with the people, and he had seized it.

Is that lordship? Is that trembling at God's Word? The fear of the Lord will keep us from compromising God's truth for the pursuit of personal gain. Then we will obey God's Word, no matter the cost, because we want to see His desires fulfilled.

Often people can read, listen and even preach the Word of God, yet live as those who do not know God's Word. There is very little change in their lives. Virtually no transformation has taken place. The psalmist describes the condition of those who attend the house of God, hear His Word and yet remain unchanged. He says, "Men who never change their ways and have no fear of God" (Ps. 55:19, NIV).

Such individuals profess that they have been saved, yet remain unchanged by God's power. They are unholy, unthankful, unloving, disobedient and unforgiving, and they exhibit other traits as well that make them no different from those who have never heard God's Word. They probably do not smoke, drink or swear like the heathen on the streets, but inside their motives are the same—these people are self-seeking. Paul described their condition as continuously learning but never able to apply the knowledge of the truth. Such people are deceived. (See 2 Timothy 3:1–7, 13.)

In the desert, the children of Israel suffered this shortsightedness of a veiled heart. The veil was called deception. They heard God's Word and saw His mighty power, yet remained very much the same. Their lack of holy fear caused their spiritual eyes to be darkened.

Without true repentance, this veil thickened to the point of blindness. The Israelites' hearts were blinded to the manner of persons they had become. While they celebrated deliverance from Egypt (the world), they lost touch with the purposes of God and drew back, even cowered, when His glorious presence was revealed. The same could happen to us if we do not heed God's warnings.

REMOVING BARRIERS

When have you taken the Lord's teachings and worked your own desires into that instruction? Ask God to lift the veil of deception from your own heart, and make the decision to move out of a state of selective obedience.

43

PRAYER

Father, lift the veil of deception from across my eyes. I want to hear Your truth and then obey it. I repent of all deception in my heart. I long to obey You with all my heart. Forgive me for only taking from the Bible what fits my needs and desires. Thank You for the forgiveness of sins through my relationship with Jesus Christ. Teach me to obey all of Your truth in the Bible with only Your desires at heart. In Jesus' name, amen.

 *Today's Light on the Path:*

1 SAMUEL 15:1–33 • 2 TIMOTHY 3:1–13

Diligent in Our Obedience

44

So we must listen very carefully to the truth we have heard, or we may drift away from it.

—HEBREWS 2:1

There is a high calling for every believer: to be conformed to the glorious image of Jesus Christ. (See Philippians 3:14; Romans 8:29.) But if we are not diligent to obey God's Word, we will unwittingly drift from the course He sets before us.

Can you imagine attempting to drive while blindfolded? You could turn on the ignition, but in no time your car would veer from your destination! It's impossible to see where you are going when you are blindfolded. Obedience to God keeps your eyes uncovered!

We are changed into what we behold. If a veil covers our spiritual eyes, then our image of the Lord becomes distorted. Jesus said, "Your eye is a lamp for your body. A pure eye lets sunshine into your soul. But an evil eye shuts out the light and plunges you into darkness. If the light you think you have is really darkness, how deep that darkness will be!" (Matt. 6:22–23).

Our eyes are the lamp that gives direction to our bodies (our being). This image of the lamp speaks not only of physical sight, but also of the eyes of the heart (Eph. 1:18). Our entire being follows the heart's perception and directions. If our eyes see the living Word of God, then our entire being will be filled with the light of God's nature. (See Hebrews 4:12–13; 1 John 1:5.) When we are continually transformed in this light of truth, we remain safe and will not drift off course.

Jesus went on to say that when an individual's eyes are focused upon evil, that person's entire being will flood with the nature of darkness. This

45

describes the darkened heart of an unbeliever. But look closely at His last statement: "If the light [which is your perception of Jesus] you think you have is really darkness, how deep that darkness will be!" (Matt. 6:23). This statement is not made to an unbeliever, but to the person who knows God's Word. The light is in Christ. Jesus is saying that if our perception is darkened or veiled due to a lack of holy fear, this darkness will actually be greater than the darkness that shrouds those who have never seen or heard the truth. (See Jude 12–13; Luke 12:47–48.)

Peter encourages us that God "has given us all of his rich and wonderful promises. He has promised that you will escape the decadence all around you caused by evil desires and that you will share in his divine nature" (2 Pet. 1:4). A share in Christ's divine nature—what a wonderful promise!

Peter explains that the fulfillment of this promise is both conditional and progressive. For he says, "We have the prophetic word confirmed, which you do well to heed as a light that shines in a dark place, until the day dawns and the morning star rises in your hearts" (2 Pet. 1:19, NKJV). The condition: Follow the exceeding great and precious promises. The progression: As we tremble and obey, then the light of His glory will grow. It begins as the strength of dawn and continues from glory to glory until it shines as the sun in full power. Proverbs 4:18 tells us, "The way of the righteous is like the first gleam of dawn, which shines ever brighter until the full light of day." In the perfect day we shall shine as the sun forever. (See Matthew 13:43.) We will not reflect His glory, but emit it! Hallelujah!

REMOVING BARRIERS

When have you actually beheld Christ's glory? As you pray, ask the Lord to shine His glorious presence upon you.

PRAYER

Heavenly Father, thank You for the rich and wonderful promises in Your Word. Empower me to hide these promises in my heart, and use these words to change my life so I'm more like Jesus. If I stumble and sin, use these promises to convict me of my sin and move me to confession and repentance.

I ask to walk in the light of Your truth and to purpose to obey You. Guard my eyes from darkness, and fill my eyes with Your light. Fill me with Your strength so I can glory in the light of Your love. Amen.

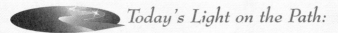 *Today's Light on the Path:*

MATTHEW 25 • ISAIAH 60

47

Removing the Log of Judgment

48

And why worry about a speck in your friend's eye when you have a log in your own? How can you think of saying, "Friend, let me help you get rid of that speck in your eye," when you can't see past the log in your own eye? Hypocrite! First get rid of the log from your own eye; then perhaps you will see well enough to deal with the speck in your friend's eye.

—MATTHEW 7:3–5

Just as a veil over our spiritual eye will distort our image of the Lord, so will a log—especially when we ignore the log in our eyes and use our spiritual "side vision" to find the specks in others' eyes. I (Lisa) probably have had enough logs in my eyes to build a cabin. My most prominent log was a tendency to be critical and to judge. Another person's speck might be a tendency to gossip or to be angry.

This scripture must be interpreted in context with the preceding scripture: "Do not judge, or you too will be judged" (Matt. 7:1, NIV). A speck may blur your vision, but a log obstructs it—and judging others is a log.

Such logs become all you see. People with "log vision" find that everywhere they look they see only the flaws of others. Sawdust is the by-product of construction using such wood logs. The sawdust of others becomes the focus. Those with "log vision" recognize in others a by-product of themselves.

Sawdust is not as obvious as specks or logs. People with logs walk about, totally unaware of their own blinders, all the while attempting to remove the various specks from the eyes of others. When you get a mental picture of it, you will see how silly and dangerous it is to think we could help anyone else with logs blinding our own eyes. No one would agree to surgery by a blindfolded surgeon.

Our purpose is not to judge others with the truths we learn, but to judge ourselves. So often it is easier to listen to the sermon and apply it to someone else, perhaps the person sitting next to us. Or to read a book for someone else. I have done it— I know. I'll read a book and think, *This is great! Boy, I know some people who really need to read this!* My mind begins to race as I scheme how I'll get each person a copy of the book or how I'll find a way to read passages from it aloud to them.

Now that's all right if I just want to share something that has already helped me. It is all right to help another when our eyes are clear. The only problem is I usually skip the "this helped me" step and leap right into the process of helping or changing others. I become so busy reading the book for others that I fail to apply its truths to my own life. Jesus said first remove the log from our own eye, and then take care of the speck in our brother's eye. When the logs are removed, we see clearly because our motives are pure.

REMOVING BARRIERS

*Take a few moments to get quiet before God and calm
your heart and mind. Are there any logs in your eyes?
Allow the Word of God to reveal them. The world is
hard to change, but you can change yourself! Ask God
to reveal areas where you can grow and deepen your
obedience to the Lord.*

PRAYER

Father, Your Word is a lamp unto my feet and a
light unto my path. It is so important that I be able
to see that light. I repent of any tendency to judge
others. Father, remove the measure of judgment
against me as I sow mercy to others. Portion Your
mercy to me as I now extend it to others.

Open my eyes and remove any logs that obstruct
my vision. I know it is Your truth that makes me free.
I realize that the discomfort I have experienced is
because I felt that it was my responsibility to change
or judge my brothers and sisters. Father, You alone
know the secrets of my heart, and I release them into
Your care. Amen.

 *Today's Light on the Path:*

JAMES 4:7–12 • 1 CORINTHIANS 4:1–5 • LUKE 6:37 •
ROMANS 14:3–4, 10–13

Section Three

REMOVE THE BARRIER
OF UNFORGIVENESS

Pathway to His Presence

coworker has taken credit for your work, or a friend has maliciously gossiped behind your back. The list of possible offenses in this life is endless. Maybe you've thought, *This time I'll forgive them—but I will never forget!*

How we handle these incidents is critical. Do you operate in forgiveness, or do you tally a mental list of wrongs? If you are keeping such a list, it will weigh down your heart and spirit and can eat away at you like cancer.

The Word of God cautions us that "all have sinned; all fall short of God's glorious standard" (Rom. 3:23). Through the death, burial and resurrection of Jesus Christ, God's Son, we have forgiveness for our sins, though we deserve death and eternity in hell. "For the wages of sin is death, but the free gift of God is eternal life through Christ Jesus our Lord" (Rom. 6:23).

We have been given the priceless and indescribable gift of forgiveness. Such a gift must never be treated as common or simply forgotten and taken for granted. When life hurts you unexpectedly, how will you respond? Will you release forgiveness, or harbor negative feelings and withhold forgiveness? If you hold back life-giving forgiveness, a root of bitterness will grow in your wounded heart (Heb. 12:15).

If anyone deserved to harbor ill feelings toward another, it was Jesus Christ. Although He was sinless, Roman soldiers scourged and beat Him unmercifully, then laid Him on a cross and pounded nails into His hands and feet. If that wasn't enough pain,

54

the soldiers lifted the cross and dropped it into a shallow hole with a bone-jarring blow. No greater method of torture existed. As Jesus hung on the cross, Luke captured His words: "Father, forgive these people, because they don't know what they are doing" (Luke 23:34).

The crowd at His feet had no relationship or belief in the Son of God. They scoffed, "He saved others . . . let him save himself if he is really God's Chosen One, the Messiah" (Luke 23:35).

Two common thieves hung on each side of Jesus. One of the thieves joined in with the crowd, telling Jesus to save Himself—and him as well. But it was the response of the other thief that touched the heart of Jesus:

> "Don't you fear God even when you are dying? We deserve to die for our evil deeds, but this man hasn't done anything wrong." Then he said, "Jesus, remember me when you come into your Kingdom."
>
> And Jesus replied, "I assure you, today you will be with me in paradise."
>
> —LUKE 23:40–43

As He hung in pain on the cross, again the Son of God released the power of forgiveness to transform a life. Jesus had reached out and touched a dying thief with eternal forgiveness.

The next few pages celebrate forgiveness. Draw life from this spiritual resource. Let it dispel the bitter disappointments of life with joy. Our model for living is Jesus Christ. As we follow Christ, He lives through us, and we are a shining example to both believers and unbelievers who cross our path. During the next five days we'll also examine the trap of unforgiveness.

God the Father longs to share with us these key truths to forgiveness. These principles increase our intimacy with the Lord. Without them, barriers will arise that will keep us from entering God's presence. Let's turn again to the pathway to His presence.

Unbridled Forgiveness From God

While knowledge may make us feel important, it is love that really builds up the church. Anyone who claims to know all the answers doesn't really know very much. But the person who loves God is the one God knows and cares for.

—1 CORINTHIANS 8:1–3

The person who loves God is the one God knows and cares for. God knows us. Without this recognition, we cannot enter into His kingdom. In a few references in the New Testament, individuals are told, "Depart! I don't know you." They knew Him, but He did not know them.

By loving God, we are transformed into the image of His Son, and therefore we are recognized as His children. God knows we can't even love Him without His help, so He has supplied a selfless love for us. "Dear friends, let us continue to love one another, for love comes from God. Anyone who loves is born of God and knows God" (1 John 4:7).

Love comes from God, not from feelings, relationships or circumstances. It is a divine impartation from our Father. "We love each other as a result of his loving us first" (1 John 4:19).

We can love Him because it is safe to do so. We will not be rejected. His love will not cease or change. It is limitless. When we look deep into the glass, we see an ever-increasing revelation of that love. The love of God frees us from fear.

"Such love has no fear because perfect love expels all fear. If we are afraid, it is for fear of judgment, and this shows that his love has not been perfected in us" (1 John 4:18).

If you are afraid, it is because you are trying to love others without first experiencing a love for God. You will always fail and fall short if you first attempt the love of others when you have not wholeheartedly pursued the love of God. In the love of God, you will find His gracious forgiveness so you can, in turn, graciously forgive. You find His love, and therefore you can love. God has forgiven you of so much. It's easy to love others when you are overwhelmed by the love of God. We have a continual need for God's mercy in our life. In fact, each day we should love Him more because we know Him more.

Often we get our eyes off of God and back onto ourselves or onto our brothers and sisters. Our vision becomes dim, and our love waxes cold. We focus on our failures at loving instead of on the source of love. Now is the time to return our love to Him. We've made the mistake of trying to love others to prove our love for Him. We need to ask Him to renew our love for Him. We need to ask Him, "Place me like a seal over your heart, or like a seal on your arm. For love is as strong as death. . . . Love flashes like fire, the brightest kind of flame" (Song of Sol. 8:6).

We have been like wayward wives who loved others and forgot our first true love. We have lavished our works, affections and strength on the "husband" of religion and forgot the love of our youth. Some no longer sense His love, but He has promised, "In a moment of anger I turned my face away for a little while. But with everlasting love I will have compassion on you" (Isa. 54:8).

The first true measure of a person's love is their trust and faith toward God. This is followed by their love for God. His love is everlasting, regardless of our faithlessness.

REMOVING BARRIERS

Focus on your love relationship with God the Father. Know where you are in your Christian walk so that love can grow. The depth of God's love is unfathomable and a source of perpetual revelation of God Himself. Take a moment and praise God for His perfect and unconditional love for you.

PRAYER

Father, thank You for Your amazing love and presence in my life. Teach me and enable me to love You more each day. Help me to show Your love to the world around me.

I praise You for Your forgiveness and compassion in my life. I ask You to forgive my sins and short-comings—those known and unknown. Renew my love relationship with You, and move me along the pathway to a deeper relationship with You. In the precious name of Jesus, amen.

 *Today's Light on the Path:*

1 JOHN 3:10–4:19 • 1 CORINTHIANS 13

The Unexpected Power

But I say, love your enemies! Pray for those who persecute you! In that way, you will be acting as true children of your Father in heaven. For he gives his sunlight to both the evil and the good, and he sends rain on the just and on the unjust, too.

—MATTHEW 5:44–45

When we were first married, John did something that really hurt me (Lisa). It happened a few times. Each time John came to me afterward and apologized. But I would reject his apology. "I'll believe you are sorry when you change!"

This response was safe for me. It meant that I did not have to extend forgiveness to John until he had proven himself worthy of it. This pattern continued for a while. Each time John hurt me, I felt more justified in withholding my forgiveness. He would apologize, and out of my hurt, I would lash out: "I knew you weren't sorry! You did it again! I don't even want to hear your apology!"

I was bitter and tormented because I had never extended forgiveness. It happened again, and now I was mad at John *and* God. I went to prayer and asked the Lord to change my husband, and here is how the Holy Spirit answered: "John will not be able to change until you forgive him."

"I don't believe he is sorry," I argued. "If he were, he would stop it! Why is everything always my responsibility? Why do I always have to be the one to change? I'm the one who is getting hurt!"

"Tell John you believe he wants to change, and that you forgive him."

God had issued some very clear directives to me without once commenting on John's behavior. I had wanted Him to judge John, and perhaps even speak to him in a dream and scare him. But God wasn't interested in my solution. Instead, He presented me with some options. Now I had the choice to obey

His command to forgive and release John, or to disobey and retain this offense. This went against everything within me, for I had been taught that the way for a person to prove he was sorry was by changing.

God was challenging me to extend mercy to John when I didn't think he had earned it. That is the beauty of mercy. It cannot be earned, and it is given when we deserve it least, because that is when we need it most.

I went to John and shared with him what God had told me. I apologized for punishing him with my unforgiveness. I had done it to protect myself but ended up hurting us both. Once I was obedient, the power of God was released into our situation, and healing and restoration took place.

It was a moment of truth for me, and I would face many more. Some of them caused me to take stock of my heart, and I discovered that I didn't always like what I found there. I sought to blame others to ease my discomfort, because then I would not be responsible for my own actions. Right?

I did this for a while, hoping it would make me feel better. I had forgotten that by bringing up the past offenses of others, I was also dredging up my own. I had forgotten also that if I held my loved ones accountable for their pasts, then God would have to hold me accountable for mine as well. Remember, He uses the same measure and method of judging us that we have used to judge others. We cannot pick and choose the application of Scripture to suit our own liking.

Jesus instructs, but He allows each individual to decide whether or not he or she will obey His Word. Jesus leads; He never forces anyone to follow Him.

REMOVING BARRIERS

When it comes to change, so often we place the blame on others instead of examining ourselves. Take a moment and ask God what needs to change in your own heart and life.

PRAYER

Lord, You are a God of mercy and grace. I realize I need this mercy and grace on a daily basis, therefore I extend it to others and accept it as my own through the blood of Jesus. I embrace Your forgiveness, and I open my heart to You. Work in my life; mold and shape me into a person who loves You and glows with the presence of Jesus. I praise You because You care about every detail of my life. Lead me farther down the pathway toward intimacy with You. In the mighty name of Jesus, amen.

 *Today's Light on the Path:*

2 PETER 1:1–15 • GENESIS 45

Plant Love and Forgiveness to Harvest Life

And then many will be offended, will betray one another, and will hate one another. Then many false prophets will rise up and deceive many. And because lawlessness will abound, the love of many will grow cold. But he who endures to the end shall be saved.

—Matthew 24:10–13, NKJV

In this section of Matthew, Jesus is teaching about the signs of the end of this age. His disciples asked, "What will be the sign of Your coming?" (Matt. 24:3, NKJV).

Many strongly believe that we are in the season of Christ's return. Never before have we seen such prophetic fulfillment in the church, in Israel and in nature. So we can confidently say that we are in the time period Jesus described in Matthew 24.

Notice one of the signs of His pending return: "Many will be offended . . ." (v. 10, NKJV). Not a few, not some, but many.

First we must ask, Who are these offended individuals? Are they Christians or just society in general? We find the answer as we continue to read: "Because lawlessness will abound, the love of many will grow cold" (v. 12, NKJV). The Greek word for love in this verse is *agape*. There are several Greek words for love in the New Testament, but the two most common are *agape* and *phileo*.

Phileo defines "a love found among friends." It is an affectionate love that is conditional. On the other hand, *agape* is "the love God sheds abroad in the hearts of His children." It is the same love that Jesus gives freely to us. It is unconditional. It is not based on performance or even whether it is returned. It is a love that gives even when rejected.

Without God we can only love with a selfish love—a love that cannot be given if it is not received and returned. However, agape loves regardless of the response. This agape is the love Jesus shed when He forgave us from the cross. So, "the many" to whom Jesus refers are Christians whose agape has grown cold.

There was a time when I did everything I could to show my love to a certain person. But it seemed that every time I reached out to love, the person slapped me back with criticism and harsh treatment. This went on for months. One day I was fed up.

I complained to God. "I have had it. Now You are going to have to talk to me about this. Every time I show Your love to this person, I get anger thrown back in my face!"

The Lord began to speak to me. "John, you need to develop faith in the love of God!"

"What do You mean?" I asked.

"He who sows to his flesh will of the flesh reap corruption," He explained, "but he who sows to the Spirit will of the Spirit reap everlasting life. And let us not grow weary while doing good, for in due season we shall reap if we do not lose heart" (Gal. 6:8–9, NKJV).

The Lord continued speaking to my heart, "You need to realize that when you sow the love of God, you will reap the love of God. You need to develop faith in this spiritual law—even though you may not harvest it from the field in which you have sowed or as quickly as you would like. In My greatest hour of need, My closest friends deserted Me. Judas betrayed Me, and Peter denied Me. I had cared for them for years. Yet I chose to forgive and die for them. They didn't ask for forgiveness, yet I freely gave it. I had faith in the

Father's love. I knew that because I had sown love I would reap love from many sons and daughters of the kingdom."

I stopped seeing it as a failure when love wasn't returned from the person to whom I was giving it. It freed me to love that person even more!

REMOVING BARRIERS

Evaluate your love relationships with God and others. Are they based on phileo *or* agape *love? What steps can you take to strengthen your agape love? Make some specific plans in this area.*

PRAYER

Lord, empower me to love You and others with unconditional love. The world loves with conditional love, yet I pray You will give me Your supernatural power to love with no strings attached—without conditions. I purpose by Your grace to sow seeds of love and forgiveness to those who cross my path today. Guide my steps into a deeper walk with You. I celebrate Your vast love for me and for the world around me that was demonstrated through the death and resurrection of Jesus.

I praise You for how You are taking my hand and leading me down the pathway to intimacy with You. I commit my plans into Your hands and ask You to fill them with love. Amen.

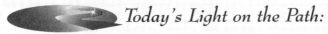 *Today's Light on the Path:*

MATTHEW 24 • GALATIANS 6

Cancellation of Your Debt

*T*hen Peter came to him and asked, "Lord, how often should I forgive someone who sins against me? Seven times?" "No!" Jesus replied, "seventy times seven!"

—MATTHEW 18:21–22

In these verses, Jesus sheds more light on the bondage of unforgiveness and offense. He was teaching the disciples how to be reconciled with a brother who had offended them.

When Peter suggested forgiving an offense seven times, he thought he was being generous. Peter liked to take things to the extreme. On the Mount of Transfiguration, this disciple said, "Lord, this is wonderful! If you want me to, I'll make three shrines, one for you, one for Moses, and one for Elijah" (Matt. 17:4). Now he thought he was being magnanimous: "I'll impress the Master with my willingness to forgive seven times."

But he received a shocking reply. Jesus blew away what Peter considered generous. "'No!' Jesus replied, 'seventy times seven!'" (Matt. 18:22). In other words, forgive as God does—without limits.

Then Jesus told a parable to emphasize His point. "For this reason, the Kingdom of Heaven can be compared to a king who decided to bring his accounts up to date with servants who had borrowed money from him. In the process, one of his debtors was brought in who owed him millions of dollars" (Matt. 18:23–24).

Jesus was emphasizing that this servant owed an impossible debt. We read: "He couldn't pay, so the king ordered that he, his wife, his children, and everything he had be sold to pay the debt. But the man fell down before the king and begged him, 'Oh, sir, be patient with me, and I will pay it all.' Then the king was filled with pity for him, and he released him and forgave his debt" (Matt. 18:25–27).

The king represents God the Father, who forgave this servant a debt that was impossible for him to pay. The debt we were forgiven was unpayable. There was no way we could ever repay God what we owed Him. Our offense was overwhelming. So God gave salvation as a gift. Jesus paid the certificate of debt that was against us. We can see the parallel between this servant's relationship to his king and our relationship with God.

> But when the man left the king, he went to a fellow servant who owed him a few thousand dollars. He grabbed him by the throat and demanded instant payment. His fellow servant fell down before him and begged for a little more time. "Be patient and I will pay it," he pleaded. But his creditor wouldn't wait. He had the man arrested and jailed until the debt could be paid in full.
>
> —MATTHEW 18:28–30

One of his fellow servants owed him a sizable sum of money—a few thousand dollars. But remember that this man was forgiven a debt of millions. That's more money than he could earn in a lifetime!

The offenses we hold against each other, compared to our offenses against God, are like a few thousand dollars compared to millions. We may have been treated badly by someone else, but it does not compare to our transgressions against God.

A person who cannot forgive has forgotten the great debt for which he was forgiven. When you realize that Jesus delivered you from eternal death and torment, you will release others unconditionally. If you have a hard time forgiving, think of the reality of hell and the love of God that saved you from it.

REMOVING BARRIERS

Are you holding offenses from relatives, neighbors or friends in your heart? Take a few moments and think about the results of unforgiveness and carrying the offenses of others. Lift those offenses and your unforgiveness into the hands of God.

PRAYER

Lord, I admit that at times it has felt good to harbor unforgiveness in my heart and not forgive another person. I have wanted them to feel badly about their hurt. Yet in my heart I know that unforgiveness is wrong. Give me greater understanding about the great cancellation of debt and the cleansing of my own sins through Jesus. Thank You for forgiving a debt that is impossible for me to repay. Now provide me this measure of Your grace to forgive anyone who offends me with a loving and free heart.

I ask for the power of Your Spirit to invade my life moment by moment. Teach me how to forgive others. I want to celebrate Your truth in my life today. In Jesus' name, amen.

 *Today's Light on the Path:*

MATTHEW 18 • 1 CORINTHIANS 6

What About Forgiveness Relapses?

But I say, love your enemies! Pray for those who persecute you! In that way, you will be acting as true children of your Father in heaven. For he gives his sunlight to both the evil and the good, and he sends rain on the just and on the unjust, too.

—MATTHEW 5:44–45

S everal years ago, someone in ministry offended me (John). The extreme offense wasn't a single experience but one of several with this person over a year and a half. Through prayer and fasting, I finally came to a place where I could pray, "Lord, I forgive him and release him from everything he has done." Immediately my burden lifted—yet it was only the beginning of my journey toward recovery.

A few months later, I had to fight off some of the same thoughts I'd had before I forgave. Finally I asked the Lord how to keep these thoughts from drawing me back into unforgiveness. I did not want to live the rest of my life holding offense at arm's length. The Lord instructed me to pray for the man who had hurt me, reminding me of those verses from Matthew 5:44–45.

So I prayed. At first it was in a dry, monotone voice, without a hint of passion. Out of obligation I would add, "Lord, bless him. Give him a good day. Help him in all he does. In Jesus' name, amen."

After a few weeks, I seemed to be getting nowhere. Then one morning the Lord impressed me with Psalm 35. I had no idea what was in Psalm 35, so I began to read. When I got halfway, I saw my situation.

> Malicious witnesses testify against me. They accuse me of things I don't even know about. They repay me with evil for the good I do. I am sick with despair.
>
> —PSALM 35:11–12

I could identify with David. In my opinion, both the man and some of his associates had rewarded me with evil for good. My soul was definitely in sorrow. God was using this psalm to point out my battle for those last few years. Then I read, "Yet when they were ill, I grieved for them. I even fasted and prayed for them, but my prayers returned unanswered. I was sad, *as though they were my friends or family*, as if I were grieving for my own mother" (Ps. 35:13–14, emphasis added).

David said that these men were trying to destroy him. They attacked him with evil when he had done nothing to merit it. David's response was not based on the actions of others. Determined to do what was right, he prayed for them as if they were his close brothers or as one grieving the loss of a mother. God was showing me how to pray for this man: "Pray the very things for him that you want Me to do for you!"

Now my prayers totally changed. No longer did I pray, "God bless him and give him a good day." My prayers became infused with life. I prayed, "Lord, reveal Yourself to him in a greater way. Bless him with Your presence. Let him know You more intimately. May he be pleasing to You and bring honor to Your name." I prayed what I wanted God to do in my own life.

Within a month of praying passionately for him, I cried with a loud voice, "I bless you! I love you in the name of

Jesus!" It was a cry from deep within my spirit. I had gone from praying for him for my own sake to praying for him for his sake. The healing was complete.

REMOVING BARRIERS

Pray for anyone who has offended you. Make a commitment to pray about this individual's concerns consistently in the weeks ahead. Ask God to do the same things for this person that you want Him to do in your life.

PRAYER

Lord, I admit that I have a recurring problem with _____. I wanted to leave these problems at the foot of the cross, but in my human frailty I've often picked up the problem and started to carry it again. I pray for _____. Touch this individual's life and deepen his or her faith walk with You. I choose to break through this relapse of unforgiveness through the power of Your grace. Thank You for filling my heart with love for You and for _____. I give my heart to You and ask You to change it. It's out of my control and in Your hands. In the mighty name of Jesus, amen.

 *Today's Light on the Path:*

MATTHEW 5

Section *Four*

FACING THE PAST WITH RENEWED HOPE FOR THE FUTURE

Pathway to His Presence

Often our past shapes who we are today. Our background, family life, training and walk with the Lord all contribute to who we are. Thanks to God's grace, we don't have to remain mired in the past. Through the power of God's Spirit, we can move forward in the present with renewed hope for our future.

In the Book of Isaiah, the Lord recounts the great miracles He preformed for the children of Israel as they escaped Egyptian bondage. Then He proclaims, "But forget all that—it is nothing compared to what I am going to do. For I am about to do *a brand-new thing.* See, I have already begun! Do you not see it? I will make a pathway through the wilderness for my people to come home. I will create rivers for them in the desert!" (Isa. 43:18–19, emphasis added).

The Lord longs to do a brand-new work in our lives. We have yet to know God as intimately as He knows us. Paul described this relationship: "And all of us have had that veil removed so that we can be mirrors that brightly reflect the glory of the Lord. And as the Spirit of the Lord works within us, we become more and more like him and reflect his glory even more" (2 Cor. 3:18).

As we grow in our knowledge of God, we escape our dim past and begin to reflect God's desires for our lives. His transforming truths are not often the easiest to embrace. They challenge our patterns of comfort. Once these patterns have been established, they are often difficult to relinquish. And God's truths also collide with religious strongholds and traditions, which are formed early and run deep.

Not all traditions are wrong, but when a person responds merely from tradition and not from his heart, he will go through lifeless motions. A person who has a religious spirit is one who has an outward form of godliness, holding fast to what God did in the past while resisting what God is doing in the present.

The Pharisees in the days of Jesus had this type of behavior. They boasted that they were Abraham's children and sons of the covenant. They claimed to be disciples of Moses. Bound to the past, they resisted the Son of God who stood in their midst. They were zealous for their traditions and style of worship. But when Jesus came, He challenged every area of comfort. The Lord Jesus made them realize that God wasn't going to fit into their box—they would have to fit into His. They resisted this change and clung to their traditions. A religious spirit breeds an elitist attitude, which will result in prejudice and eventually hatred and betrayal if not checked.

For us to change and make the transition from one level of glory to the next we must be willing to leave our comfort zones and pursue the way of the Spirit of the Lord. This path will cause new life to spring forth.

Lisa and I are excited about the truths God will illuminate as you study the scriptures in the pages that follow. They will give you some new insights into releasing the bonds of your past and trusting God for the present and the future. Though you may be facing circumstances that look humanly impossible, hold on to the promise of God that

Jesus spoke: "Everything is possible with God" (Mark 10:27).

These next few devotional selections will help you along the pathway into God's presence.

Escape Our Past

If you keep looking steadily into God's perfect law—the law that sets you free—and if you do what it says and don't forget what you heard, then God will bless you for doing it.

—JAMES 1:25

few years back, I (Lisa) had the honor of being one of the daytime speakers for a national conference. I had spoken the previous day and was getting ready to attend a luncheon for all the speakers before my afternoon session. I was especially excited about this opportunity to meet so many women of God all at once! I could listen to their conversations and ask questions. On top of this, I didn't have any of my children with me. I was alone—with female adults!

As I headed to lunch, the Spirit arrested me: "Go out to your car. I want to talk to you."

I felt like a child being sent to her room. Why now? Couldn't I just go in for a little while and then come outside?

I didn't sense a very positive response to my suggestion from the Holy Spirit, so I turned around and returned to my big red truck. I climbed in a little reluctantly. There I was, in high heels and a dress, sitting in a truck in the church parking lot. By now, all the other speakers would be meeting and greeting. It reminded me of when I nursed my babies and spent most social events shut away in the confines of a back bedroom.

I decided to shake this perception of punishment. Some of my most treasured memories were of the peaceful faces of my nursing babies. I stilled my thoughts and listened.

Immediately I sensed God's presence. I grabbed pen and paper to scrawl down any truths He would impart. I flipped through my Bible for the references that confirmed His voice.

I don't know how long I was out there. It seemed

like moments in the richness of His presence and fellowship. I didn't even want to leave when it was time for me to go inside. That afternoon I was delivering a message called "Escaping Your Past." I had written about this subject in my first book and was pretty confident about my message. In the stillness of the truck, God expanded my afternoon message.

He began by telling me the American church has enshrined her past. The past has been used as an excuse or justification for present behavior. When we make excuses for ourselves by drawing from the past, it is idolatry. An idol is what we give our strength to or draw our strength from.

Some people in the church spend themselves in the research of their own pasts, searching for a reason to the riddle of their lives. They may think their past justifies their present, but the truth is that the past will never justify their future. This is deception.

We are not the focus. Our focus is the perfect law of liberty. This law will give us the freedom we now search for in our pasts. We are forgetful when we only hear the Word and do not obey it. Part of obedience is applying God's truth to our lives and circumstances.

REMOVING BARRIERS

Have you ever used your past to excuse your present behavior? How? Ask the Holy Spirit to give you insight into your heart in this regard.

PRAYER

Lord God, I don't want to be mired in the past. I choose to walk away from it and embrace the future You have for me. I want to grow daily to be more like You. As I look into the mirror I will focus on beholding You and the truth of Your Word. Transform me as I behold You. Because You have already forgiven my past, I too release it and step into the freedom You have already purchased for my life. Thank You that *my past is not my future.* In the mighty name of Jesus, amen.

 *Today's Light on the Path:*

PHILIPPIANS 3

87

Is God in Control?

88

O Lord my God, you have done many miracles for us. Your plans for us are too numerous to list. If I tried to recite all your wonderful deeds, I would never come to the end of them.

—Psalm 40:5

When Joseph's brothers sold him into slavery, it probably never crossed Joseph's mind that his suffering and hardship were part of God's preparation process. Joseph was learning obedience, and his brothers were skillfully wielded instruments in the hand of God.

Joseph may have regarded his dreams as a confirmation of God's favor upon his life. He had not yet learned that authority is given to serve, not to set an individual apart. Often in such periods of training we focus on the impossibility of our circumstances instead of the greatness of God. As a result we get discouraged and feel the need to blame someone, so we look for the one we feel is responsible for our despair. When we face the fact that God could have prevented our entire mess—and didn't—we often blame Him.

This perhaps kept ringing through Joseph's mind: *I have lived according to what I know of God. I've not transgressed His statutes or nature. I was only repeating a dream God Himself gave me. And what's the result? My brothers betray me, and I'm sold as a slave! My dad thinks I'm dead, so he'll never come to Egypt to find me.*

To Joseph, the bottom line was his brothers. They had thrown him into this dungeon. How often do we fall into the same trap of assigning blame? For example:

"If it weren't for my wife, I would be in the ministry. She has hindered me and ruined so many of my dreams."

"If it weren't for my parents, I would have had a normal life. They are to blame for where I am today.

Why do others have normal parents and I don't?"

"If my mom and dad hadn't gotten divorced, I would have been much better off in my own marriage."

"If it weren't for my former husband, my kids and I wouldn't have all this financial trouble."

"If it weren't for that woman in the church, I would still be in favor with the leaders. With her gossip, she has destroyed me and any hope I had of being respected."

The list is endless. It is easy to blame everyone else for your problems. I want to emphasize the following point: Absolutely no man, woman, child or devil can ever remove you from God's plan for your life! If you lay hold of this truth, it will set you free. Only one person can get you out of the will of God—and that is you!

God holds your destiny. Joseph's brothers tried hard to destroy the vision that God gave him. They thought they had ended it for Joseph and wanted no chance that he would ever succeed. But in God's plan, Joseph ruled Egypt. And the brothers? Ironically, Joseph's brothers became the patriarchs of Israel! God had promised Abraham that they would bring forth a nation. Through one of them the Lord Jesus would eventually come!

Joseph kept his heart free from offense, and the plans of God were established in his life and in the lives of his brothers as well. As we experience life and move along the pathway to His presence, we can rest in the assurance that God's plans for us are too numerous to mention. With this assurance, we can face the future and leave the past behind us.

REMOVING BARRIERS

Do you assign blame to others—or even God—for your present difficulties? How are you responsible for your own failures or actions in the past? How are you responsible for your future?

PRAYER

Lord, You stand outside of time—where there is no past, present or future. You have seen my steps and experiences in the past. Now take those experiences and use them in my life. I want those past experiences to mold and shape my life so that I become more like Jesus. If I've tried to blame my present circumstances on someone or someplace or some situation, I'm wrong and confess my failure in this area. I ask that You will reveal Your plans for my life and that I will have the daily courage to follow Your leading. Thank You for Your careful guidance. In Jesus' name, amen.

 *Today's Light on the Path:*

PSALM 37

Beyond Our Shortsightedness

Godliness leads to love for other Christians, and finally you will grow to have genuine love for everyone. The more you grow like this, the more you will become productive and useful in your knowledge of our Lord Jesus Christ. But those who fail to develop these virtues are blind or, at least, very shortsighted. They have already forgotten that God has cleansed them from their old life of sin.

—2 PETER 1:7–9

The Bible promises that the more we grow in faith, virtue, knowledge, self-control, perseverance, godliness, brotherly kindness and love, the more we will grow in our intimacy with Him. Each of these measures can be increased by the use and exercise of our faith. We are also warned that "those who fail to develop these virtues are blind or, at least, very shortsighted" (2 Pet. 1:9).

Nearsighted and blind people have a hard time seeing things accurately. I (Lisa) know—I'm nearsighted. Without the help of my glasses, I do not recognize the form of my own husband until he is within twenty feet of me. Impaired eyesight causes us to lose our edge and insight. The nearsighted only notice the obvious. Often the obvious overshadows the eternal.

This shortsighted condition makes us forgetful. "Where did I leave my keys?" If the item is not right in front of us, we quickly forget it. Peter said this condition will cause us to forget we have been cleansed. When this knowledge is lost, we will begin to make excuses.

Why would anyone go to the trouble to explain away something for which they were no longer accountable? If an individual remembered that he or she has been cleansed, that person would simply say, "Oh, that was before I was made new."

When we do not obey the truth that has been clearly revealed, we will deceive ourselves (James 1:22). Our hearts again condemn us if we attempt to justify our sins by the works of the flesh and the psychology of man. Let's go back to the purpose of salvation. Was it not to restore us to God through the remission of sins and the removal of our past?

When I stand before God, I will stand alone, as an individual. Each of us will be judged for what we alone have done. That is why I needed a Savior. I had lived a life that could not stand the scrutiny and presence of a holy God. I became a Christian when I realized that I was sinful and God was holy. The two could never touch, but Jesus became my Mediator.

Job described his need for a Savior this way: "If only there were a mediator who could bring us together" (Job 9:33).

We have Someone who mediates between God and us. Picture this: The Book of Life is opened, and the judgments written against us are read aloud for all to hear. In the presence of this holy Judge, our sins are gross and the list extensive and far-reaching. We fear that we are not forgivable.

Our only hope is our glorious Advocate, the Judge's only Son. We weep and tremble in the silence that proceeds the pronouncement of our judgment: "You are guilty as charged."

Then our Advocate steps forward and pleads our cause. "Father, You are just to pronounce her guilty.

She knew this day would come, and she traded her sin-riddled life for My lordship. She has been My servant. My death satisfies the written judgment against her. The sins she has committed are under the covering of My blood."

"Forgiven," the Judge

declares. Now we are free! Imagine the relief and joy! Once and for all eternity we have been judged worthy of citizenship in God's kingdom—not because of what we did or because of the lives we lived, but because of what Jesus did. His righteousness is beyond question, and it has been assigned to us!

REMOVING BARRIERS

Are you caught up in the details of life? Has the eternal picture of life escaped your view? Take a few moments to celebrate God's forgiveness of your past actions, then ask God to help you refocus your perspective on the eternal, long-range view of eternity.

PRAYER

Heavenly Father, I ask You to quiet the voices in my head and heart that condemn me and pull me back into my shortsighted thinking from the past. Help me to celebrate how You've forgiven my past. Thank You for the one who is the Mediator between God and man: Jesus, the Christ. Give me the wisdom and understanding to grow each day to become more like Jesus. I celebrate the lordship of Christ in my life. Amen.

 *Today's Light on the Path:*

1 CORINTHIANS 15 • ROMANS 3

95

Let Go of the Old

96

No, dear friends, I am still not all I should be, but I am focusing all my energies on this one thing: Forgetting the past and looking forward to what lies ahead, I strain to reach the end of the race and receive the prize for which God, through Christ Jesus, is calling us up to heaven.

—PHILIPPIANS 3:13–14

P hilippians 3:13–14 instructs us to forget what is behind. (This means all of it—the good, the bad and the ugly.) It exhorts us to strain for what is ahead, releasing the load of our past. That is the only way we can have the necessary strength to persevere to our goal.

Are you in Christ? Then let go of the old because it is gone; a new way of living has been prepared for you. Use your gift of faith to step into this new life. Let go of your past, because your past is not your future.

God is the Lord of our future. He has plans for us. He is always planning ahead so we don't have to. All we have to do is trust Him and learn His ways. His ways are higher and wiser, and He clearly tells us to forget our past.

How many marathon runners carry backpacks? If they started with one, it would soon be dropped in order to lighten their load so they could finish their race. Marathon runners compete in the lightest apparel possible and carry only what is necessary for their journey. The marathon runner knows he must conserve all his strength for the race at hand.

We also run a race. It is not only a physical race, but a spiritual one. That is what makes this race different. "The way of the righteous is like the first gleam of dawn, which shines ever brighter until the full light of day" (Prov. 4:18). As we walk the path, it becomes clearer and more distinct.

Some of you are running with backpacks filled with stones because you are trying to bring your past into the future. Others of you are looking back. Maybe you are afraid your future will be like your past. Now is the time to put the past to rest. When we excuse our behavior by our past, we say, "I've earned the right to be this way because of what was done to me." This attitude betrays the presence of unforgiveness in our hearts. Forgiveness is the very foundation of the gospel. Without forgiveness, there is no remission of sin. Unforgiveness will keep us bound to our past. "Stop judging others, and you will not be judged. Stop criticizing others, or it will all come back on you. If you forgive others, you will be forgiven" (Luke 6:37).

Unforgiveness inevitably causes us to lose sight of our own need of forgiveness. We have God's promise that if we forgive, we will be forgiven. It is when we don't forgive that the weight of our own sins comes back to bear down on us. The forgiveness of God is the very force that releases us from our past. We can even release others, for "if you forgive anyone's sins, they are forgiven. If you refuse to forgive them, they are unforgiven" (John 20:23). But remember—by not forgiving others, we are also not forgiven. Some of us have withheld forgiveness as a form of punishment, when in the end, we were only punishing ourselves. Is it worth it?

REMOVING BARRIERS

Have you accumulated stones of your past, packed them up and attempted to carry them into your future? In your mind, one by one get rid of each stone, and then let go of the past. In faith, trust your future to Jesus.

PRAYER

Lord God, sometimes I feel as if I'm a marathon runner who is loaded with a backpack of stones. I'm trying to carry my past into my future. In the name of Jesus, I choose by Your grace to remove this weight of my past and run toward You. I don't want to look behind me, but rather to strain ahead with Your strength and blessing.

If I'm holding on to any feelings of unforgiveness toward others, I release these feelings into Your hands. I want to forgive others and celebrate the forgiveness that I have received from You through Christ. Thank You for the gift of eternal life. Amen.

 *Today's Light on the Path:*

2 CORINTHIANS 5

Fast to Release the Past

100

The LORD will guide you continually, watering your life when you are dry and keeping you healthy, too. You will be like a well-watered garden, like an ever-flowing spring.

—ISAIAH 58:11

The Bible tells us the story of a widow woman named Anna, who was very old. She holds a very important historical significance:

> She was now eighty-four years old. She never left the Temple but stayed there day and night, worshiping God with fasting and prayer. She came along just as Simeon was talking with Mary and Joseph, and she began praising God. She talked about Jesus to everyone who had been waiting for the promised King to come and deliver Jerusalem.
>
> —Luke 2:37–38

I challenge you to go before our Father and ask Him, by the power of the Holy Spirit, to reveal any areas in your life for which you need to fast.

The one who fasts must do so with the right motivation. Jesus often reproved the Pharisees for their religious, pious fastings done only for the attention it brought to them. Matthew 6:16 advises us to not be like the hypocrites.

Hypocrite is another name for impostor. An impostor is one who deceives others by using assumed character or false pretenses. The Pharisees pretended to fast unto the Lord when it was really done for the accolades of man. Their focus was their pious religious appearance, and their reward was the recognition of man. They wanted to be great among men. But they received nothing from God's hand. You must choose between the reward of man or the reward of God. The religious fast is rewarded by man, while the broken and contrite are rewarded by God. Jesus continued:

101

But when you fast, comb your hair and wash your face. Then no one will suspect you are fasting, except your Father, who knows what you do in secret. And your Father, who knows all secrets, will reward you.

—MATTHEW 6:17–18

If we are not hungry for God, it is because we have allowed our souls to be satisfied or satiated with other things. One morning when I was praying, I sensed the need for more of a hunger for God. I asked God to impart this hunger in me. At the time, I was recording my prayers in my journal. I waited for a response from God.

As fast as I could write, He answered me. He showed me that I was the one responsible for my hunger level. He told me that if I wasn't hungry, it was because I was already full—filled with the cares of this world and filled with the pleasures and distractions of this world. He said that if I wanted to hunger in the midst of the abundance of things, I would need to fast—fast the things that would distract, comfort or distress me.

God wants to be an integral part of our lives every day, not just when we are on the mountaintop spiritually. I have had to develop a listening ear, one that can hear amid the din and noise of a full household.

This may shock you, but most of the time on my knees has been spent emptying my

102

heart and repenting. Once this is done, I can usually hear God's voice whenever He desires to speak to me.

REMOVING BARRIERS

God can use fasting to cleanse you of the past and impart godly insights into your daily life. Ask God to show you areas for fasting.

PRAYER

Lord, I long to hear Your voice in my life. Use fasting to release me from the cares of my past and present. I want to focus on You and how You are leading me along a pathway to a deeper relationship with You. Honor the desire of my heart to be faithful to You. Through the Holy Spirit, reveal areas of sin in my life, and lead me to areas that I can fast for Your glory. In the strong name of Jesus, amen.

 *Today's Light on the Path:*

ISAIAH 58

A NEW GENERATION TO REFLECT GOD'S GLORY

Pathway to His Presence

The prophet Malachi wrote in the final book of the Old Testament:

> "Look! I am sending my messenger, and he will prepare the way before me. Then the Lord you are seeking will suddenly come to his Temple. The messenger of the covenant, whom you look for so eagerly, is surely coming," says the LORD Almighty. "But who will be able to endure it when he comes? Who will be able to stand and face him when he appears? For he will be like a blazing fire that refines metal or like a strong soap that whitens clothes. He will sit and judge like a refiner of silver, watching closely as the dross is burned away. He will purify the Levites, refining them like gold or silver, so that they may once again offer acceptable sacrifices to the LORD."
>
> —MALACHI 3:1–3

God is raising up a generation of people who will manifest His glory, not their own—a people made in His image, who walk in His character. The Word says, "But in a great house there are not only vessels of gold and silver, but also of wood and clay, some for honor and some for dishonor. Therefore if anyone cleanses himself from the latter [iniquity], he will be a vessel for honor, sanctified and useful for the Master, prepared for every good work" (2 Tim. 2:20–21, NKJV).

Notice there are two types of vessels, honorable and dishonorable. The Greek word for dishonor, *atimia*, is defined as "dishonor, reproach, shame, vile." The Greek word for honor is *time*, which is defined as "precious." Through purging or cleansing, our lives are refined and made free from impurities. Paul talks about gold and silver. Their refining processes have similarities. In order to simplify, let's briefly discuss gold.

Gold has a beautiful yellow color, emitting a soft metallic glow. It is widely distributed in nature but always found in small quantities. Rarely is gold found in a pure state. In a pure state, gold is soft, pliable and free from corrosion and other substances. The parallel in our lives before God is that a pure heart before God is like pure gold.

Through the refiner's fire, gold is purified. The dross or the impurities are removed. The apostle Peter talked about this refining process in our lives as we learn about God's character, saying, "So be truly glad! There is wonderful joy ahead, even though it is necessary for you to endure many trials for a while. These trials are only to test your faith, to show that it is strong and pure. It is being tested as fire tests and purifies gold—and your faith is far more precious to God than mere gold. So if your faith remains strong after being tried by fiery trials, it will bring you much praise and glory and honor on the day when Jesus Christ is revealed to the whole world" (1 Pet. 1:6–7).

Through trials and tribulations we go through God's refining fire. The heat of this fire separates our impurities from the character of God in our lives.

As we draw into God's presence the Lord will change our character to reflect that of Jesus. During the next five days along the pathway to His presence, we will examine major barriers that have kept so many from drawing closer. If we are to be a generation that reflects God's glory, we will have to learn to remove these obstacles. Change is never easy. In fact, in our own limited strength it is impossible. But as we cooperate with the power of God's Spirit through obedience, we will see a transformation take place that many long for but cannot obtain in their own strength. The greatest benefit will be that we will develop a more intimate relationship with God. Let's turn the page and continue our journey.

What's Fair?

Again, the Kingdom of Heaven can be illustrated by the story of a man going on a trip. He called together his servants and gave them money to invest for him while he was gone. He gave five bags of gold to one, two bags of gold to another, and one bag of gold to the last—dividing it in proportion to their abilities—and then left on his trip.

—Matthew 25:14–15

The "it's not fair" barrier can loom large before us. Just as Addison learns below, we must learn that fairness is not a prerequisite to God's glory.

"If all of us are created equal, then it isn't fair!" This wail of protest would usually float into my kitchen. Sometimes it was a toy dispute: "I had it first!" or "He got more!" At other times it was a game or sports conflict: "He cheated!" or "It's my turn!"

Whenever possible, I (Lisa) would act as though I had not heard. I wanted to remain uninvolved. I would pause to determine just how far it would escalate. Would it be a minor scuffle involving only words? Or was it an opportunity for bloodshed?

With four boys, often a single day will hold many such skirmishes. I try to stay out of these disagreements, first, because I always hope that the children will resolve them, and second, I dread stopping what I am doing to walk upstairs or go outside to referee them.

When my oldest son, Addison, began grade school, his perception of fairness expanded to encompass an entirely new dimension. He became the self-appointed administrator of justice. This job description included seating arrangements, "You sat next to Dad last night, and tonight is Alexander's turn." Or, "I'm oldest, so I should sit in the front seat of the car." It spread to the domain of food, where fairness was scrutinized according to his preferences. If it was a portion of ice cream, it was not fair to give them all the same amount. After all, he was the oldest! If it was beans, it wasn't fair to give him more, because he didn't like them.

The fairness checks and balances bred clashes whenever there was a perceived violation. This all began to wear thin on me. It seemed everything I asked him wasn't fair, and everyone he knew wasn't fair! One night in response to my request for him to help pick up the TV room, he protested, "It's not fair! I didn't play with all these toys, and I always end up putting away more!"

I took a deep breath and sat him down. I let him know that I fully understood how he felt. I shared how often I felt it wasn't fair that I had to clean up messes that I didn't make and wash clothes I hadn't soiled.

He smiled and patted me. "Let's make the babies pick up all the toys, and we'll go read a book!"

I could see I wasn't getting anywhere. He needed a new perspective. I asked him this question: "Was it fair that Jesus died on the cross when He had done nothing wrong?"

He looked perplexed, and his tone changed. "No."

"God didn't ask Jesus to die because it was fair. He did it because it would be just. Jesus died to fulfill the punishment for man's sin. Addison, life is not fair, but God is just."

It was one of those quiet and precious moments when you see in your child's eyes a truth implanted. You know beyond a shadow of a doubt that your child has understood what you've said.

He quietly nodded his blond head, hugged me and

began picking up the toys, calling to his brothers, "Here, you guys, big brother will show you how!"

Let Jesus show you how to recognize His justice—it's the path to His glory.

REMOVING BARRIERS

Throughout every day, the people of the world are demanding their "rights." Consider the difference between fairness and justice. Which has a higher value for you? In prayer, leave the justice and fairness issues into God's capable hands.

PRAYER

Lord God, thank You for the grace, mercy and truth You shower on me each and every day of my life. If I received what was fair or what I deserved for my sins, I would be eternally punished. Yet through the resurrection of the Lord Jesus, You provided a way by which I can spend eternity in Your presence. Help me to operate in love with those people who cross my path today. Instead of pushing for fairness or justice—which is a natural human tendency—give me a heart of love and compassion through the power of Your Spirit. I want to live in Your mercy rather than experience Your justice. Thank You for caring about the details of my life. Amen.

 *Today's Light on the Path:*

JOHN 3 • PHILIPPIANS 2

Revenge: The Trap

*Never pay back evil for evil to any-
one. Do things in such a way that
everyone can see you are honorable.*

—ROMANS 12:17

Holding on to an offense of unforgiveness is like holding a debt against someone. When another person offends us, we often feel they are indebted to us or owe us something.

Our court system exists to avenge wronged or injured parties. Lawsuits result from people trying to satisfy their debts. When a person has been hurt by another, human justice says, "They will stand trial for what they have done and pay the penalty if found guilty."

This is not the way of righteousness. "Dear friends, never avenge yourselves. Leave that to God. For it is written, 'I will take vengeance; I will repay those who deserve it,' says the Lord" (Rom. 12:19).

It is unrighteous for us as the children of God to avenge ourselves. But that is exactly what we are seeking to do when we refuse to forgive. We desire revenge and watch for an opportunity to carry it out. We withhold forgiveness until the debt is paid to our satisfaction, determining for ourselves what is acceptable as compensation. When we seek to correct the wrong done to us, we set ourselves up as judges. God is the just judge. He will repay according to righteousness. If someone has done wrong and genuinely repents, Jesus' work at Calvary erases the debt.

You may argue, "But I was wronged, not Jesus!"

Yes, but you have forgotten the offense you committed against Him. He truly was an innocent victim. He bore no guilt while each one of us has sinned and was justly condemned to die. Each one of us has broken the laws of God, and these transcend the laws of the land. If justice was served, all of us would deserve death at the hand of the highest court in the universe.

You may have done nothing to provoke the injury you incurred at the hand of another. But if you contrast what was done to you with what you've been forgiven of, there is no comparison. It would not even put a dent in the debt you owed! If you feel cheated, you have lost your concept of the mercy extended you.

Under the Old Testament covenant, if you trespassed against me, I had legal rights to retribution. The Law reigned supreme. Jesus had yet to die to set us free. Look how He addresses New Covenant believers:

> You have heard that the law of Moses says, "If an eye is injured, injure the eye of the person who did it. If a tooth gets knocked out, knock out the tooth of the person who did it." But I say, don't resist an evil person! If you are slapped on the right cheek, turn the other, too. If you are ordered to court and your shirt is taken from you, give your coat, too. If a soldier demands that you carry his gear for a mile, carry it two miles. Give to those who ask, and don't turn away from those who want to borrow."
> —MATTHEW 5:38–42

Jesus eliminates any gray areas for grudges. In fact, He says our attitude is to be so far removed from avenging ourselves that we are willing to open ourselves to the possibility of being taken advantage of again.

When we seek to correct the wrong done to us, we set ourselves up as judge. We must make room and give place to the Lord, the just Judge. He rewards righteously. Only He avenges in righteousness. Along the pathway to His presence, we can rest in the assurance that God is our righteous and just Judge. Vengeance belongs to Him alone—it is never ours.

REMOVING BARRIERS

Whenever we are wronged, our natural inclination is to lash out and to fight back. Have you been "wronged" recently? What was your response? How can you return the evil done to you with love and goodness? It is the way that often amazes others and testifies about Christ.

PRAYER

Heavenly Father, Your Son, Jesus, was truly innocent—yet He died for my sins. Thank You for paying the debt I never could. In this world, it's so tempting to fight back on every front, but You have delivered me from the power of this world's system. I renounce any tendency or attitude toward revenge and purpose to guard my heart. Grant me a supernatural measure of Your love so I can extend mercy to others. I commit any revenge issues into Your hands. Thank You for Your promise to reward the righteous. In the mighty name of Jesus, amen.

 *Today's Light on the Path:*

1 JOHN 1–2

Release All Bitterness

*The Lord made this covenant with
you so that . . . no root among you
would bear bitter and poisonous fruit.*

—DEUTERONOMY 29:18

I (John) was ministering on the subject of offenses at a church in Florida. A woman came to me and said she had forgiven her ex-husband for all he had done. As she listened to me talk about releasing offenses, she realized that she still did not have peace inside and was very uncomfortable.

"You still have not forgiven him," I told her gently.

"Yes, I have," she said. "I have cried tears of forgiveness."

"You may have cried, but you still have not released him."

She insisted that I was wrong and that she had forgiven him. "I don't want anything from him. I have released him."

"Tell me what he did to you," I asked.

"My husband and I pastored a church. He left me and our three boys and ran away with a prominent woman in the church." Tears formed in her eyes. "He said he'd missed God by marrying me because it was God's perfect will for him to marry the woman he ran away with. He told me that she was an asset to his ministry because she was much more supportive than I. He said I was a hindrance and that I was critical. He blamed the entire marriage breakup on me. He has never come back and admitted that any of it was his fault or doing, nor has he apologized."

This man was obviously deceived and had greatly wronged his wife and family. She had suffered much pain due to his actions and was waiting for him to pay off his debt. This debt had nothing to do with financial support—her new husband provided this for her. She wanted her ex-husband to admit to being wrong and to acknowledge that she had been right.

We are admonished by the apostle Paul, "Remember, the Lord forgave you, so you must forgive others" (Col. 3:13). And, "Be kind to each other, tenderhearted, forgiving one another, just as God through Christ has forgiven you" (Eph. 4:32).

I gently explained to this woman, "You won't forgive him until he comes to you, admits he was wrong, that it was his fault not yours, and then asks for your forgiveness. This is the unfulfilled payment that has kept you bound."

Tears streamed down her face. What she wanted seemed small compared to all the pain he had brought to her and her children. But she was in bondage to human justice. She had set herself up as a judge, claiming her right to the debt and waiting for payment. This offense had hindered her relationship with her new husband. It had also affected her relationship with all male authorities because her former husband had been her pastor as well.

The writer of Hebrews admonished us to "pursue peace with all people, and holiness, without which no one will see the Lord: looking carefully lest anyone fall short of the grace of God; lest any root of bitterness springing up cause trouble, and by this many become defiled" (Heb. 12:14–15, NKJV).

Bitterness is a root. When roots are nursed, watered, protected, fed and given attention, they increase in depth and strength. If not dealt with quickly, roots are hard to pull up. The strength of an offense grows with the passage of time. The Bible warns us that a person who does not pursue peace by releasing offenses will eventually become defiled. That which is precious inevitably becomes corrupted by the vileness of unforgiveness. On the pathway to His presence, we are challenged to pursue peace.

REMOVING BARRIERS

Search deep within your heart for the root of bitterness. Are you presently bound by the weight of unfulfilled payments or promises? Release these unfulfilled expectations into God's capable hands and pursue the peace that leads to God's glory.

PRAYER

Lord God, I admit to the weight and bondage of unfulfilled expectations and broken promises. I release every unfulfilled expectation and promise into Your hands. May Your Word become a hedge round about my heart to guard me from bitterness. Fill my heart with Your love, and may peace guard me whenever someone crosses my path. Lead me along the narrow pathway into Your presence. Amen.

 *Today's Light on the Path:*

EPHESIANS 4–5

121

Remain Stubborn or Be Willingly Broken

Anyone who stumbles over that stone will be broken to pieces, and it will crush anyone on whom it falls.

—Matthew 21:44

J esus is the stumbling stone, and His breaking process could be compared to a trainer breaking a war-horse. A horse is not fit for battle until its will is broken. Though it may be stronger, swifter and more gifted than the other horses, it cannot serve until its will is subjected. To be broken does not mean becoming weakened. It means that your will is completely submitted to the will of your master. In the horse's case, its master is the rider. If the horse is successfully broken and trained, it can even be trusted in war. In the heat of battle when arrows or bullets fly, this animal will not flinch. As axes, swords and guns are raised in war, it will not deviate from its master's desires. It remains firmly submitted to its master, without attempting to protect or benefit itself.

This breaking process is unique to each individual and is determined by the Lord Himself. He is the only one who knows when this process is complete. I remember His breaking process in my life. All too often I fully believed I was ready and fit for service. I would declare with confidence, "I am fully submitted to Your authority. I know I am ready for the ministry to which You have called me." Yet the wise in heart knew I wasn't yet broken. Sure enough, I'd go through another bout, all the while struggling for my rights.

Just as with horses, our breaking process deals with submission to authority. This authority can be God's direct or delegated authority. It does not matter, for all authority is from Him. (See Romans 13:1–2.) God knows the perfect process for each of us.

God set up two kings who illustrate the breaking

process: Saul and David. Saul represented the people's desire in a king, accurately reflecting that for which their rebellious hearts cried out. Saul never went through a breaking process. His life is a tragic example of an unbroken man who was given authority and power. Saul used his authority and God-given gifts to further his own purposes.

On the other hand, David was God's choice. He went through several years of breaking and training. The majority of it came at the hand of his corrupt leader, King Saul, the authority under which God had placed David. He was severely tested, but when God saw that His vessel was broken and submitted, He placed him in authority. Even though he made mistakes, David always remained tender and faithful to the authority of God.

In contrast, Saul obeyed God when it fit in with his plans or agenda but would sway when it didn't. He would carry the word of the Lord with his own motives attached. Saul was confronted by the prophet Samuel for disobedience and rebuked with these words: "Stubbornness is as iniquity and idolatry" (1 Sam. 15:23, NKJV).

Why is stubbornness compared with idolatry? Stubbornness is direct insubordination to God's authority. A person decides that he is master of himself and therefore serves the idol of self-will.

Our democratic society is a breeding ground for insubordination. Because of this we have lost sight of what it means to submit to authority. True submission never wavers. Yet today we only submit when we agree. If authority goes against our will or direction, we disobey or grudgingly go along with it until a better option presents itself. This makes us especially vulnerable to deception and counterfeit ministry.

REMOVING BARRIERS

As we submit our will to the Lord, He molds our attitudes and protects us against the fiery darts of Satan. Are there areas in your life that you are resisting giving to God? Do you give your burdens to the Lord and then immediately take them back? Make a commitment to give God your total service and complete submission.

PRAYER

Lord God, I've fought this concept of brokenness and found false security in my lack of submission. I admit my own stubborn ways in trying to manage in my own power. I've turned from Your authority and attempted to handle situations in my own strength. Forgive me for my stubborn heart and for failing to turn to You for every need.

I ask You by the power of Your Spirit to teach me about submission and brokenness. On the pathway to Your presence, I long to be a vessel that is fit for service. As a part of that training process, I acknowledge that brokenness is a part of the journey. I'm willing, and into Your hands I give my life. Thanks for Your gentleness and love. Amen.

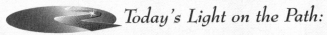 *Today's Light on the Path:*

ROMANS 13 • MATTHEW 8:5–13

Loose Pride and Put On Humility

Pride leads to arguments; those who take advice are wise.

—Proverbs 13:10

As believers, rather than battle for our rights or privileges we need to battle against the foe of pride. One time my wife and I were having intense fellowship (quarreling). In the heat of it, the Lord spoke to me: "Your pride is being exposed." I was immediately convicted as Proverbs 13:10 came into my mind.

God continued, "John, any time you and Lisa fight, you'll find pride lurking somewhere, and you must deal with it."

One may argue, "What if I know I'm right?" Jesus answered this question, "Come to terms quickly with your enemy" (Matt. 5:25). By refusing to defend yourself, one, if not both, of the following things will happen: First, you lay down pride, which will open your eyes to recognize flaws in your own character that went undetected previously. Second, if you are right, you will still be following the example of Christ by allowing God His rightful place as judge of the situation.

"For God is pleased with you when, for the sake of your conscience, you patiently endure unfair treatment. . . . This suffering is all part of what God has called you to. Christ, who suffered for you, is your example. Follow in his steps. He never sinned, and he never deceived anyone. He did not retaliate when he was insulted. When he suffered, he did not threaten to get even. He left his case in the hands of God, who always judges fairly" (1 Pet. 2:19, 21–23).

This is our calling: to follow Christ's example, who suffered when He was not at fault. This precept wars against the natural mind, since its logic appears absurd. However, the wisdom of God proves that humility and obedience make room for God's righteous judgment. Defense, correction, vindication or whatever other response is appropriate should proceed from the hand of God, not from man. An individual who vindicates himself does not walk in the humility of Christ. No one on earth possesses more authority than Jesus, yet He never defended Himself.

Jesus was accused of a complete lie! There was not a morsel of truth in what they accused Him of. Yet He did not correct his accusers or defend Himself. His behavior caused the governor to marvel at His composure. He had never seen such behavior from a man. (See Mark 15:1–5.)

Why didn't Jesus defend Himself? It was so that He could remain under His Father's judgment and thus His protection. When we refuse to defend ourselves we are hidden under the hand of God's grace and judgment. There is no safer place.

"Come to terms quickly with your enemy before it is too late and you are dragged into court, handed over to an officer, and thrown in jail. I assure you that you won't be free again until you have paid the last penny" (Matt. 5:25–26).

According to this parable you will be made to pay whatever your accuser demands as restitution. You will be left helpless and at his mercy. The greater the offense he bears toward you, the less mercy he will extend to you. He will exact every last penny of your debt.

Pride would say, "Defend yourself." Jesus said, "Come to terms quickly with your enemy." In so doing, you lay down pride and make God the judge of the situation.

"Therefore, anyone who becomes as humble as this little child is the greatest in the Kingdom of Heaven" (Matt. 18:4).

When we humble ourselves by obeying God's Word, then His favor, grace and righteous judgment rest upon us. This attitude is hard to develop in our quick, convenient and easy society. We often lack the stamina required to patiently endure. God's deliverance always comes, but often it is different than what we expect—His deliverance comes with great glory! Humility is the only road to true and enduring success.

REMOVING BARRIERS

Examine your personal battle with pride. Do you easily defend yourself, or do you follow Christ's example of humility? Purpose to follow Jesus closer.

PRAYER

Father God, it's natural to desire to defend myself. But by the power of the Holy Spirit, empower me to follow Christ's example. I purpose to walk this difficult yet safe path to Your presence and to remain in the safety of Your grace. When I'm wronged, I commit the offense into Your hands. You are strong and able to handle any difficulty. Provide me with Your answer and direction. In Jesus' name, amen.

 *Today's Light on the Path:*

1 PETER 2:13–23 • MARK 15:1–5 • ROMANS 12:19–21

Section *Six*

GROWING IN
GOD-CONSCIOUSNESS

Pathway to His Presence

he world wants you to build up "self." It entices you to build your life, business or ministry with bricks of your own making: through the strength of your personality, through worldly programs and by clever techniques. It also tempts you to build by manipulation or to control through intimidation. But if you flatter to gain position or build by tearing others down through criticism or gossip, then everything gained will be lost. Whatever you build will be burned.

Paul wrote, "Stop fooling yourselves. If you think you are wise by this world's standards, you will have to become a fool so you can become wise by God's standards. For the wisdom of this world is foolishness to God. As the Scriptures say, 'God catches those who think they are wise in their own cleverness'" (1 Cor. 3:18–19).

The focus of this world's wisdom is self. "If you are bitterly jealous and there is selfish ambition in your hearts, don't brag about being wise. That is the worst kind of lie. For jealousy and selfishness are not God's kind of wisdom. Such things are earthly, unspiritual, and motivated by the Devil" (James 3:14–15). In God's eyes, any area of your life in which your motive is self-seeking is considered as wood, hay or straw. Regardless of how much it appears to help others or operates in the name of the Lord, or the involved amount of time sacrificed, it all burns.

Envy breeds competition in the church, and the fear it brings causes division. We begin to "power position" ourselves in order to keep our domain safe. This posturing may cost us friends, integrity or most importantly, our relationship with God. Often, even ministers are driven by the concerns of position, title or salary to the neglect of seeking God's heart on behalf of the people. These weights choke a leader's love for God's people, causing ministries to become self-serving. Such ministers strive for success to fill voids that only God can fill.

Many, however, are seeking God's heart. The more they seek Him, the more they appear to decrease. They cry, "Lord, the more I seek You, the more I go down, not up." But He answers, "Dig deeper. 'Whoever comes to Me, and hears My sayings and does them, I will show you whom he is like: He is like a man building a house, who dug deep and laid the foundation on the rock' (Luke 6:47–48, NKJV)."

God separates those who wait on Him from those who build with the tools of "hype" or "programs." Promotion will come to those who are watching and waiting for Him to come to His temple. God says, "At the time I have planned, I will bring justice. . . . For no one on earth—from east or west, or even from the wilderness—can raise another person up. It is God alone who judges; he decides who will rise and who will fall" (Ps. 75:2, 6–7).

As we continue along the pathway to His presence, the consciousness of self must decrease so that our consciousness of God might increase. During the next five days, we'll examine how selfish actions become barriers to intimacy with the Lord. In the pages that follow, you will learn to fill your mind and heart less with self and more with God. Such a process is significant and another step closer to intimacy with the Lord along the pathway into His presence.

Which Standard for Obedience— Yours or God's?

136

Stop judging others, and you will not be judged. For others will treat you as you treat them. Whatever measure you use in judging others, it will be used to measure how you are judged.

—MATTHEW 7:1–2

I f we judge, we will be judged. One day while drying my hair, I (Lisa) was thinking about, and judging, a friend who had hurt me. I told myself that I always knew she was that way and that I was staying away from her!

This person had hurt me repeatedly. Over the years I had flitted in and out of a friendship with her. One minute we were the best of friends, the next minute we were enemies without any apparent cause for the shift in sentiment. Later she would float back into a relationship with me, only to have the cycle play itself out again. Gossip was inevitably involved, and I decided I was finally through with her!

After making this determination, I expected to feel freedom, but instead I felt grieved as the Spirit checked me. I defended my position: "I'm right to judge her. She is this way!"

Immediately I sensed the Spirit of God question me. "Is that what you want Me to say about you?"

I was stunned. After all, I wasn't the issue here! What did I have to do with this? I was talking about her. The Holy Spirit continued, "When you judge someone you are saying they are never going to change, and therefore you don't have to be reconciled with them. If you judge them, then I must judge you. Do you want me to say, 'Lisa is never going to change'?"

The apostle James wrote, "God alone, who made the law, can rightly judge among us. He alone has the power to save or to destroy. So what right do you have to condemn your neighbor?" (James 4:12). I had presumed to know someone else's heart, and when I judged this person I ended up feeling grieved because I was placing myself under judgment. God alone is judge, and He will share this position with no one. I knew this woman's actions, but I could only guess at her motives.

Although I thought my information was accurate, it was incomplete at best. It is important to note that this conversation never hit the airwaves—it took place only in my head. I never intended to publicly denounce her, but as prosecutor and judge I had pronounced her guilty in the biased court of my heart.

As I saw the truth, I wanted to repent. But I was concerned that my repentance might lead me back into an unhealthy relationship. Before praying, I protested, "God, it's true! This cycle keeps happening."

The Holy Spirit gently encouraged me, "I did not say you have to fellowship with her or that your assessment was totally incorrect—only that your reaction to it is wrong."

It was then that I realized it is possible to be right and still be wrong. I needed to separate this woman's actions from her motives. It was reasonable to decide that her actions warranted my caution in all future interactions. I would need to exercise God's wisdom in my relationship with her, but I was not to set myself up as judge over her.

"For there will be no mercy for you if you have not been

merciful to others. But if you have been merciful, then God's mercy toward you will win out over his judgment against you" (James 2:13).

Although I deserve judgment, I need mercy. If I want mercy, I must therefore be merciful, because only mercy triumphs over judgment.

REMOVING BARRIERS

Whom have you judged? Go before God's throne today and release him or her from that judgment. When others wrong you, the hurt caused by them can become your test. Ask God for grace to pass the test.

PRAYER

Heavenly Father, thank You for the undeserved mercy that triumphed over judgment in my life through Jesus Christ. I confess that at times I have been quick to judge friends, coworkers, neighbors—even people on the street. Through the power of Your Spirit, give me a heart filled with mercy and one free from judging others.

Thank You for the gentle way You lead me down the pathway to Your presence. I pray that as I plant seeds of mercy, I will grow closer with You. In the name of Jesus, amen.

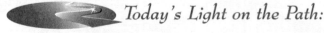 *Today's Light on the Path:*

JAMES 4 • MATTHEW 7

Counting the Cost

140

But don't begin until you count the cost. For who would begin construction of a building without first getting estimates and then checking to see if there is enough money to pay the bills? Otherwise, you might complete only the foundation before running out of funds. And then how everyone would laugh at you!

—LUKE 14:28–29

xamine your motives. Are you a true disciple of Jesus Christ, or do you desire to follow Him only if it is within certain limits that you set? Do you stay within your own boundaries, far from the borders of self-sacrifice? Could these boundaries keep you from the paths that Jesus walks and eventually disqualify you? (See 2 Corinthians 13:5.)

To decide whether or not to follow Jesus, we must first know the cost. Following Jesus requires nothing less than your entire life. Listen as Jesus outlines this to the multitudes who desired to follow Him:

> If you want to be my follower you must love me more than your own father and mother, wife and children, brothers and sisters—yes, more than your own life. Otherwise, you cannot be my disciple. And you cannot be my disciple if you do not carry your own cross and follow me. . . . So no one can become my disciple without giving up everything for me.
>
> —LUKE 14:26–27, 33

This is what it costs to endure to the end. The Book of Revelation says that those who overcome do not love their own lives, even unto death. (See Revelation 12:11.) Unfortunately, that would not be an accurate description of the church in America today.

I could give many examples of Christian men and women who still own their lives. Once when I was pastoring, a young lady came to me complaining, "Pastor John, I have such a terrible self-image. Please pray for me to have a better self-image."

I looked at her and said, "That's your problem!"

She was baffled. She expected a long counseling session with prayer at the end. She was also expecting me to be nice and sweet in order to help her feel better about herself. My reply shook her. But it is the truth that sets us free—not talking about our problems without dealing with their root.

I questioned her, "Where do you find references to self-esteem or a good self-image in the Bible? Jesus said that in order to follow Him you must die! Dead people don't have image problems! Have you ever seen a dead person sit up in a casket and say, 'Hey! Why did you put me in this outfit? I don't like it! And why did you style my hair like this? What are people going to think?' The person is dead, and he or she couldn't care less about such things, even if they were placed in a paper sack in that casket. Dead people have no image problem."

I wanted to show her that self-esteem and a good self-image are not in the Bible. Feeling good about yourself is not a requirement for loving and following Jesus. Her focus was on the temporary, not the eternal.

We cannot serve God only when we feel good about ourselves, when we are excited or when everything is going our way. We call people who behave this way "fair-weather friends." Now there are fair-weather Christians who are unwise. Eventually, they will have to face something that will not fit into their parameters. If they are not prepared, they will quit. In their hearts they will have given up their pursuit of God.

The love of God knows no limit. If we are to walk with Him, we must remove our own limitations. Removing those limits will lift another barrier along the pathway to His presence.

REMOVING BARRIERS

For a few moments, examine your motives for following Jesus Christ. Are you determined to follow through both the joy and the pain? In a spiritual sense, remove any limitations that you've set for God. Pursue love in your relationships, and ask God to deepen your intimacy with Him.

PRAYER

Lord God, I don't want to be a fair-weather Christian who only follows You within safe parameters. I've counted the cost of discipleship and understand that Jesus paid a high price for my freedom and life. I long to follow You each day with my whole heart. In the power of the Spirit, I release any limitations that I've set for God. I want to pursue love in all of my relationships.

In advance, God, I acknowledge and am grateful that You are able to do exceedingly abundantly above all I can ask or think. Thank You, heavenly Father, for teaching me about this step along the pathway to intimacy. In Jesus' name, amen.

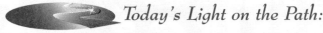 *Today's Light on the Path:*

LUKE 14 • MATTHEW 16:13–27

Walls of Protection

144

It's harder to make amends with an offended friend than to capture a fortified city. Arguments separate friends like a gate locked with iron bars.

—PROVERBS 18:19

An offended brother or sister is harder to win than a fortified city. In Solomon's day strong cities had walls around them. These walls assured the city of protection. They kept unwelcome inhabitants and invaders out. Those considered a threat to the city's health or safety were barred from the entrance.

When hurt, we construct walls to safeguard our hearts and prevent future wounds. We become selective, denying entry to any we fear will hurt us. We filter out anyone who we think owes us something. We withhold access until these people have paid their debts in full. We open our lives to only those we believe to be on our side.

Yet, often those we consider to be on our side are also offended. So instead of helping us, they help stack additional stones on our existing walls. Without our knowledge these walls of protection become a prison of offense. Soon we are not only cautious about who comes in, but we are also afraid to venture outside the walls of our fortress.

The focus of offended Christians turns inward and introspective. We guard our rights and personal relationships carefully. Our energy is consumed with making sure no future injuries occur. If we don't risk being hurt, however, we cannot give unconditional love. Unconditional love gives others the right to hurt us.

Love does not seek its own, but when people are hurt they become more and more self-seeking and self-contained. In this harsh climate, the love of God waxes cold. A natural example of this is the two seas in the Holy Land. The Sea of Galilee freely receives and gives out water. The Dead Sea takes water in, yet never gives it out. The living waters from the Sea of Galilee become dead when mixed with the hoarded waters of the Dead Sea. Love and life do not grow and flourish unless they are freely released.

An offended Christian takes life in, but because of fear cannot release it to flow into others. As a result, it is not long before the life that does come in turns stagnant within the prison walls of the offense. The New Testament describes these walls as strongholds.

"We use God's mighty weapons, not mere worldly weapons, to knock down the Devil's strongholds. With these weapons we break down every proud argument that keeps people from knowing God. With these weapons we conquer their rebellious ideas, and we teach them to obey Christ" (2 Cor. 10:4–5).

These strongholds create set patterns of reasoning through which all incoming information is processed. Although originally erected for protection, they become a source of torment and distortion because they war against the knowing or knowledge of God.

When we filter everything through past hurts, rejections and bad experiences, it becomes impossible to believe God. We cannot believe He means what He says. We doubt His goodness and faithfulness, since we judge Him by the standards set by man in our lives. But "God is not a man, that he should lie" (Num. 23:19). "'My thoughts are completely different from yours,' says the Lord. 'And my ways are far beyond anything you could imagine'" (Isa. 55:8).

Offended people will be able to find

Scripture passages to back their positions, not realizing that they are incorrectly dividing God's Word. The knowledge of God's Word without love is a destructive force because it puffs us up with pride and legalism. (See 1 Corinthians 8:1–3.) This causes us to justify our actions rather than repent of our unforgiveness, which creates an atmosphere in which we can easily be deceived. Knowledge without the love of God leads to deception.

REMOVING BARRIERS

When you are offended, how do you react? Do you respond in love, or do you build a wall of protection around yourself? How can you break down your walls of protection and reach out with God's love and restoration?

PRAYER

Father, I don't want to build walls of protection that will inevitably imprison me. I purpose to live with a confidence and boldness of Your love and care. If I've offended a brother or sister, touch my spirit and make me aware of that offense. Then help me to reconcile that relationship. I want to build and encourage those people who cross my path—not offend them. If others use the Bible in their own defense, help me to love them with Your mercy. In the strong name of Jesus, amen.

 *Today's Light on the Path:*

JOHN 15

Eternal Truth for Eternal Results

148

So we have stopped evaluating others by what the world thinks about them. Once I mistakenly thought of Christ that way, as though he were merely a human being. How differently I think about him now! What this means is that those who become Christians become new persons. They are not the same anymore, for the old life is gone. A new life has begun!

—2 CORINTHIANS 5:16–17

ternal truths produce eternal results; temporal, or temporary, truths produce temporary results. To eradicate a lie you must go back to the truths that existed before the lie. Adam and Eve had grasped at equality with God. They tried to be like God apart from God. If you believe lies, then you become afraid of truth. Turning from the truth to a lie causes the light in us to become darkness. We lose sight of the eternal and become limited to the obvious. "Self" lives in the realm of the seen, the obvious and the earthly. The consciousness of self is a direct result of the Fall.

I find it amazing that the Bible contains no physical description of Adam or Eve. Their appearance and age are not an issue. We do not find physical descriptions of any individuals until after Adam and Eve have left the garden. Only then were men and women defined by age, children, labor and accomplishments. Occasionally we find a person described in terms of his or her relationship with God. But these are isolated instances and always set apart from the rest. The lives of such people are highlighted uniquely in the unfolding plan of God for mankind.

Sarai, or Sarah, is the first individual to whom a physical description is assigned. Abraham feared the godless culture that surrounded him and his family. Afraid these evil men would kill him and take his wife, he asks Sarai to lie in order to protect him:

> As he was approaching the borders of Egypt, Abram said to Sarai, "You are a very beautiful woman. When the Egyptians see you, they will say, 'This is his wife. Let's kill him; then we can have her!' But if you say you are my sister, then the Egyptians will

149

treat me well because of their interest in you, and they will spare my life."

—GENESIS 12:11–13

After the description of John the Baptist in the Scriptures, it appears the need for physical descriptions once again becomes less important. The emphasis switches from the outward and natural appearance to the hidden and eternal person.

At one time, Jesus had walked among His disciples and other believers on this earth as the Son of man. But now He is in heaven, and it is impossible to know Him according to natural terms. We now learn of Him by the Spirit, through the Scriptures. He is progressively revealed, not as the Son of man but as the Son of God.

Jesus' disciples had known Him as the natural man, but now He is revealed as the Eternal One. Paul admonished the believers to adopt this same view of each other—to look beyond the earthly and obvious to glimpse the eternal—that "Christ lives in you . . ." (Col. 1:27). This caused him to say, "He died for everyone so that those who receive his new life will no longer live to please themselves. Instead, they will live to please Christ, who died and was raised for them. So we have stopped evaluating others by what the world thinks about them. Once I mistakenly thought of Christ that way, as though he were merely a human being. How differently I think about him now!" (2 Cor. 5:15–16).

When we turn to Christ, the

shroud of death is stripped away, and we can glimpse the eternal once again. It is a process involving the retraining of our minds and wills. Instead of serving self, we must now subject and submit self once again to the Creator. To lose an awareness of self we must gain an awareness of God.

REMOVING BARRIERS

Are you caught up in the temporal shroud of self or the eternal truths of God? Take a few moments to evaluate what fills your mind and heart every day. How can you focus more on God and less on selfish preoccupations?

PRAYER

Heavenly Father, please forgive any tendency I have toward the mastery of self. You said I was to take up my cross, deny myself and follow You. Lord, for too long I have not denied myself. I have been over-whelmingly conscious of myself. I have lived to protect and provide for myself. Please forgive me. I renounce the fallen nature that seeks to serve self, and I ask You to teach me to serve You. I want to become increasingly conscious of Your will and ways, and less and less conscious of my own will and ways. Restore my sight. Open my eyes and let me glimpse again the eternal and turn away from the sensual and earthbound. I avert my eyes from myself and turn them toward You. In Jesus' name, amen.

 *Today's Light on the Path:*

JOHN 6

151

Avoid Gossip

152

Wrongdoers listen to wicked talk;
liars pay attention to destructive words.

—PROVERBS 17:4

The Bible tells us that it is wrong to listen to wicked talk. As you listen to it, your own soul is defiled by what you hear. Unknowingly, you begin to watch for the discussed attributes or character flaws in the accused individual. Amazingly, your eyes are open, and you can see clearly what had been hidden before. You think it is because you are more discerning now. No, it's because you are more suspicious.

Suddenly, whenever you hear that individual's name mentioned, your mind sings the chorus of accusations and complaints you heard earlier. Soon you are wrestling with your own critical thoughts toward that person.

Every time I (Lisa) gossiped, I was grieved and vowed never to do it again. This was a constant source of frustration for me. I knew in my heart that it was wrong, and I did not want to do it, yet it seemed impossible to stop. I repented of one scenario only to be caught up in another. It got to the place where I asked God to isolate me until I was able to rise above this pattern or stronghold in my life.

Why had a stronghold been established in my life, and why was it so hard to overcome? Gossip is rooted in unbelief and watered by fear. Paul tells us in 2 Timothy 1:7 that fear is a spirit, but unbelief is a condition of the heart. Therefore we could certainly call gossip a heart condition. We fall prey to gossip when we are afraid to trust God to uphold us in truth. No matter how complex or unique our situation is, if we are honest we will find fear and unbelief at the root.

We refuse to forgive for fear of being hurt again. So we stand guard over past offenses. In doing so, we prove that we doubt God's ability to heal our past and protect our futures.

We malign others because we believe our worth is tied to theirs. We're afraid that if they look good we'll look bad by comparison. This reveals that our self-worth is not founded in Jesus Christ.

We are jealous because we do not believe that God is just. We are afraid He actually plays favorites and honors people instead of faith and obedience. We must remember, anything we receive is by grace and faith in God's goodness.

"Some people make cutting remarks, but the words of the wise bring healing" (Prov. 12:18). Gossip is speaking reckless or careless words that wound. The only way to heal the wounds is to speak words in response that contain wisdom and promote reconciliation. We are not to answer in the same manner that the information was brought to us. For example, never agree with the one gossiping by adding your own story about the offender also. This does not promote healing, but it widens the breach.

We are instructed: "When arguing with fools, don't answer their foolish arguments, or you will become as foolish as they are" (Prov. 26:4). The Book of Proverbs also says, "Disregarding another person's faults preserves love; telling about them separates close friends" (Prov. 17:9). These verses are referring to a hurt or wound from someone close to us. We must develop the wisdom and discernment necessary to answer with words of life. I have found that Proverbs provides an excellent source of wisdom by which to govern my heart.

By studying Proverbs, we will not only be able to answer with wisdom, but will also rightly divide our own thoughts and motives. This will carry over when we go to others with our grievances.

REMOVING BARRIERS

It is difficult to safeguard yourself from gossip, but it helps if you ask yourself these questions:

Why are they telling me this?

Are they confessing their reaction to an offense, or are they just repeating it to influence me?

Have they gone to the individuals who offended them?

Are they asking me to go with them so that restoration can take place?

Am I in a position to help them?

PRAYER

Lord God, I repent of the gossip I have either originated or listened to. I ask You to guard my eyes and ears. Break down the stronghold of gossip in my life. I admit that in my own strength, it's impossible to conquer these habits—yet "nothing is impossible with God." Help me to remove any root of bitterness and to immediately cast wicked thoughts from my mind. Place Your hedge of protection around my mind and heart. In the mighty name of Jesus Christ, amen.

 *Today's Light on the Path:*

EPHESIANS 4:20–5:2 • PHILIPPIANS 4

DRAWING CLOSER AS
YOU FEAR THE LORD

Pathway to His Presence

At the close of the Old Testament, the prophet Malachi wrote, "Then those who feared the LORD spoke with each other, and the LORD listened to what they said. In his presence, a scroll of remembrance was written to record the names of those who feared him and loved to think about him" (Mal. 3:16). The Lord is watching those whose hearts are faithful to Him in holy fear. He records their names in His book of remembrance and has confirmed that their deepest heart's desire will be fulfilled.

The fear of the Lord is a subject impossible to fully disclose, no matter how many books are written about the subject. It is a progressive and continual revelation, just as the love of God is. We are admonished, "Be zealous [passionate] for the fear of the LORD all the day" (Prov. 23:17, NKJV). We cannot draw too close.

The fear of the Lord is also difficult to define. It encompasses an amazingly broad spectrum like its counterpart, the love of God. Therefore the definition offered here is partial and merely a launching point in this revelation, for words cannot describe the inner transformation of the heart. We will grow in the revelation of God throughout eternity. Proportionately, the revelation of His love and our holy fear of Him will expand.

The fear of God encompasses, but is not limited to, respecting and reverencing Him, for we are told to tremble at His presence. Holy fear gives God the place of glory, honor, reverence, thanksgiving, praise and preeminence that He alone deserves. (Notice that it is what He deserves, not what we think He deserves.)

When God holds this preeminent position in our hearts, we will esteem His desires over and above our own, hating what He hates and loving what He loves, as we tremble in His presence and at His Word.

Now hear this and meditate on it: *You will serve whom you fear.*

If you fear God, you will serve Him. If you fear man, you will serve man. You alone can choose. The following five devotions are a study in the fear of the Lord. Make the decision today to fear and honor God above all else in your life. The fear of the Lord provides for us the secret entrance to a closer and more intimate relationship with our heavenly Father. It is another step closer on the pathway to His presence.

An Ever~Deepening Reverence

But now you must be holy in everything you do, just as God—who chose you to be his children—is holy. For he himself has said, "You must be holy because I am holy." And remember that the heavenly Father to whom you pray has no favorites when he judges. He will judge or reward you according to what you do. So you must live in reverent fear of him during your time as foreigners here on earth.

—1 PETER 1:15–17

Peter walked with Jesus and witnessed this judgment. Later he wrote the words on the previous page with inspiration and heartfelt admonishment. Notice that he does not say "live in love." Yes, we are to live in love, for without it we have nothing! Apart from His love we cannot even know the Father's heart. Earlier in this very epistle, Peter comments on the love that should burn in our hearts for the Lord, saying, "You love him even though you have never seen him" (1 Pet. 1:8). We are called to have a personal love relationship with our Father, but Peter is quick to add the balance—the fear of God. Our love for God is limited by a lack of holy fear. Our hearts are to shine with the light and warmth of both flames.

Paul did not walk with Jesus on earth but met Him on the road to Damascus. He exhorted believers as follows: "Therefore, my beloved, as you have always obeyed, not as in my presence only, but now much more in my absence, work out your own salvation with fear and trembling" (Phil. 2:12, NKJV). In fact, this phrase "fear and trembling" is used three times in the New Testament to describe the proper relationship between a believer and Christ.

We must remember both of these unchangeable attributes: "God is love" and "God is a consuming fire" (1 John 4:8; Heb. 12:29). Because of God's love, we can have confidence when we approach Him. The Bible adds that we must come before Him in an acceptable manner. How? With reverence and godly fear. (See Hebrews 12:28.)

In one of the services during a week of meetings in Kuala Lumpur, Malaysia, I trembled at God's holy presence. That day I sensed the presence of the Lord fill the building in several different waves, and numerous people laughed as His joy flowed. This continued for ten to fifteen minutes.

After this, I heard the Lord say, "I am coming in one last wave, but it will be different than the others." I kept silent and waited. Within a minute a very different manifestation of God's presence permeated the building. It was awesome and almost frightening. Yet I was drawn to it. The atmosphere became charged. The same people who had been laughing only moments earlier began to weep, wail and cry. Some even cried out as though they were on fire. However, these were not the tormented screams of demonic activity.

As I paced the platform, I thought, *John, don't make one wrong move or say one wrong word—if you do, you're a dead man.* I'm not certain that would have happened, but this thought relays the intensity I felt. Later I thought of Ananias and Sapphira. (See Acts 5:1–11.) I knew irreverence could not exist in this awesome presence.

We left the meeting shrouded in awe of God's presence. One man who was mightily touched by His presence said to me afterward, "I feel so clean inside." I agreed, for I felt purged as well. Later I found this scripture: "The fear of the LORD is clean, enduring forever" (Ps. 19:9, NKJV). In the pathway to His presence, we must fear God.

REMOVING BARRIERS

Reflect on the dual nature of the Father—He is a holy God to be both feared and loved. Worship the Lord today for who He is. Ask Him to impart holy fear into your heart as you enter His presence. Allow His holiness to deepen your love for Him.

PRAYER

Father God, make me into a holy vessel just as You are holy. Change my heart and mold me into someone who understands the fear of the Lord yet loves You with an ever-deepening love. Thank You that because of the blood of Jesus I can enter the holy of holies and stand before You. Cleanse my mind and heart today as I live and work in the world. I want to be a radiant witness of Your love and Your grace in my life. Use me to draw others to a saving faith in Jesus. I praise You that You are teaching me little by little how to proceed along the pathway into Your presence. In the name of Jesus, amen.

 *Today's Light on the Path:*

ACTS 5

163

Godly Fear Tested

164

Later on God tested Abraham's faith and obedience. "Abraham!" God called. "Yes," he replied. "Here I am." "Take your son, your only son—yes, Isaac, whom you love so much—and go to the land of Moriah. Sacrifice him there as a burnt offering on one of the mountains, which I will point out to you."

—GENESIS 22:1–2

When Abraham was ninety-nine years of age his wife became pregnant, and their promised son, Isaac, was born! Can you imagine the joy Abraham and Sarah experienced after waiting so many years? Can you imagine the love they had for this promised child?

Time passed, and this relationship grew as father and son became very close. The life of this boy meant more to Abraham than his own. His great wealth was nothing in comparison to the joy of this son. Nothing meant more to Abraham than this precious son given to him by God. Then God tested Abraham as recorded in the verses on the previous page.

Can you imagine Abraham's shock at hearing these words? Never had he dreamed that God would ask such a hard thing of him. He was stunned. Father and son were so close. After all the years of waiting for this priceless young man, God had asked for more than even Abraham's own life— He had asked for his heart. It made no sense.

But Abraham knew that God did not make mistakes. There was no denying what God had already made clear. There were only two options for a covenant man: obey, or break covenant. To break covenant was not even a consideration for this man of faith, because he was so immersed in godly fear.

We know it was a test, but Abraham did not. We seldom realize that God is testing us until we are on the other side of it. It may be possible to cheat on a university test, but no one can cheat on the exams God gives. If we have not studied and done our homework by purifying our hearts and cleansing our hands, we will not be able to pass God's tests, no matter how clever we are!

If Abraham's descendants had known the outcome of what God was doing in the desert of testing, they would have responded differently. Abraham had something different in his heart, something his descendants lacked.

God once asked me (John) to give up something I thought He had given me. It was something that meant more to me than anything else. I had desired it for years. It was the opportunity to work for a world-renowned evangelist, one I dearly loved.

My wife and I had been offered positions on staff as assistants to this man and his wife. Not only did I love this man, but I also saw it as God's opportunity to bring to pass the dream He had implanted deep within me—that I might preach the gospel to the nations of the world.

I fully expected that God would want me to say yes to this wonderful offer, but He made it clear that I was to turn it down. I wept for days after refusing the offer. I knew I had obeyed God, yet I did not understand why He had asked such a hard thing of me. After weeks of bewilderment, I finally cried out, "God, why did You make me put this on the altar?"

He quickly answered my cry: "To see if you were serving Me or the dream." Only then did I understand that I had been tested. In the midst of it, I had not realized what He was doing. All that kept me from going my own way was my love for God and my fear of Him.

REMOVING BARRIERS

Has God asked you to place a dream or desire into His hands? It is evidence of our faith when we trust God for the His ultimate guidance and plan for our lives.

PRAYER

Lord, though You have not asked me to sacrifice my only son, like Abraham I do realize I've placed certain dreams and desires before You. Thank You for the example of Abraham and his enduring trust— even when he did not see any results. Like Abraham, at times it feels as if I am in a holding pattern while I await the fulfillment of my dreams. By the fear of the Lord and the continual revelation of Your love, teach me during the times of waiting. I choose to see them as an opportunity for obedience and a time to demonstrate my trust in You. I long to serve You each day. I know Your plans for me are perfect. Reveal them in my life and in Your perfect time. In the precious name of Jesus, amen.

 *Today's Light on the Path:*

GENESIS 22

God's Boldness

168

For God has not given us a spirit of fear and timidity, but of power, love, and self-discipline.

—2 TIMOTHY 1:7

Have you ever been intimidated? The goal of intimidation is to make us give up our authority, which renders our gifts inoperative. Then we are reduced to operating in our own limited strength and ability. Usually our position changes from offensive to defensive. Then, aware that we are vulnerable, we retreat even further to what is comfortable and safe.

So, if intimidation lulls the gift asleep, what wakes it up? Boldness. But can an intimidated person apprehend boldness?

Boldness comes from the virtues of power, love and soundness of mind. True boldness comes from God and is fueled by godly virtue. Boldness that is fueled by God's character awakens the gifts in our lives.

Some people do not have virtue behind their boldness. They know the right things to say, and they act confidently when faced with little or no opposition. But their strength does not run deep. It is superficial. Their bold face is a mask for pride, arrogance or ignorance. Their roots are shallow, and eventually a strong enough storm will expose them. When the weather is good, you can't see how deeply a tree is rooted. But under the winds of adversity it will either be uprooted or proven strong.

David knew the power of God because he knew God. This boldness enabled David to fulfill his destiny and rule righteously. Let's look at his younger years.

David was the eighth son of Jesse of Bethlehem. His three older brothers served in the army under King Saul. The Philistines had gathered their army against Israel. Daily their champion "Goliath stood

169

and shouted across to the Israelites, 'Do you need a whole army to settle this? Choose someone to fight for you, and I will represent the Philistines. We will settle this dispute in single combat! If your man is able to kill me, then we will be your slaves. But if I kill him, you will be our slaves!'" (1 Sam. 17:8–9).

Ordinarily the Israelites might have considered this option over war, but Goliath was no regular soldier. According to some accounts he was over ten feet tall. To put this in perspective, look at any basketball goal. His head would have measured a couple of inches above the rim!

Now David, who tended sheep, was sent by his father to bring supplies to his three older brothers. David must have wondered, "Have they forgotten who's on our side? He is not challenging us. He is challenging God!"

David boldly demanded, "Who is this pagan Philistine anyway, that he is allowed to defy the armies of the living God?" (1 Sam. 17:26). The air was thick with confrontation. David's brother, Eliab, now bold with pride and anger, attacked David's character, not the problem facing Israel.

When a person is intimidated, he looks for an escape, a release of pressure. Eliab accused David of conceit and wickedness. Eliab thought only of himself, and he assumed David was the same way. But David was a man after God's heart. He was not proud but humble before the Lord.

People who have strong personalities will use intimidation to make a lie look like the truth. You must stay in the Spirit to overcome the strength of such attacks. Eliab, the eldest, seemed to have the characteristics of a great leader and warrior. But as God taught Samuel, "Don't judge by his appearance or height . . . the LORD doesn't make decisions the way you do! People judge by outward appearance, but the LORD looks at a person's thoughts and intentions" (1 Sam. 16:7). On our pathway into His presence, the Lord examines our hearts more than our outward experiences.

REMOVING BARRIERS

Have you found yourself intimidated recently? Ask God to reveal situations where intimidation is hindering your gifts. Remember, boldness in the Lord awakens God-given gifts. Ask God to anoint you with fresh boldness to break the chains of intimidation.

PRAYER

Lord, infuse my life with Your boldness. Like David, I long to be a person after Your own heart. I purpose to step into Your power and strength, no more to be lulled into inaction through intimidation. I choose to conquer intimidation so I can shine Your love on my family, friends, neighbors and coworkers. As I walk in the Spirit of might and boldness, use my talents and gifts for Your service. Teach me to fear and love You alone. In Jesus name, amen.

 *Today's Light on the Path:*

1 SAMUEL 17

Choose Whom You Will Fear

172

Who are those who fear the Lord? He will show them the path they should choose. They will live in prosperity, and their children will inherit the Promised Land.

—Psalm 25:12–13

Many in the church do not understand the fear of the Lord. This is unfortunate because it is a vital part of a triumphant Christian life. Isaiah prophesied concerning Jesus, "His delight is in the fear of the LORD" (Isa. 11:3, NKJV). His delight should be ours!

We are told the fear of the Lord is the beginning of wisdom and the beginning of knowledge of Him. (See Proverbs 1:7; 2:5; 9:10.) It will prolong our days, because Proverbs 10:27 says, "Fear of the LORD lengthens one's life, but the years of the wicked are cut short." We are warned that no one will see the Lord without holiness, which is perfected by the fear of the Lord. (See Hebrews 12:14; 2 Corinthians 7:1.) And this is just a sampling of what the Bible says about the fear of the Lord.

The only way to walk totally free from intimidation is to walk in the fear of the Lord. The Bible says, "Those who fear the LORD are secure" (Prov. 14:26). This security or strong confidence produces the boldness we need to go God's way rather than man's way. Let's examine the differences between the fear of God and the fear of man.

First, what is the fear of God? It includes, but is more than, respecting Him. Fearing Him means to give Him the place of glory, honor, reverence, thanksgiving, praise and preeminence He deserves. (Notice that it is what He deserves, not what we think He deserves.) God holds this position in our lives when we esteem Him and His desires over and above our own. When we fear the Lord we will hate what He hates and love what He loves, trembling in His presence and at His Word.

173

On the other hand, to fear man is to stand in alarm, anxiety, awe, dread and suspicion, cowering before mortal men. When entrapped by this fear we will live on the run, hiding from harm or reproach, constantly avoiding rejection and confrontation. We become so busy safeguarding ourselves and serving men that we are ineffective in our service for God. Afraid of what man can do to us, we will not give God what He deserves.

The Bible tells us, "The fear of man brings a snare" (Prov. 29:25, NKJV). A snare is a trap. Fearing man steals your God-given authority, causing His gifts to then lie dormant in you. You feel powerless to do what is right because the empowering of God is inactive.

God's Word admonishes, "Listen to me, you who know right from wrong and cherish my law in your hearts. Do not be afraid of people's scorn or their slanderous talk . . . So why are you afraid of mere humans, who wither like the grass and disappear? Yet you have forgotten the LORD, your Creator" (Isa. 51:7, 12–13). When we please men to escape reproach, we forget the Lord. We depart from His service. Paul said, "If I were still trying to please people, I would not be Christ's servant" (Gal. 1:10).

You will serve and obey whom you fear! If you fear man, you will serve him. If you fear God, you will serve Him. You cannot fear God if you fear man, because you cannot serve two masters! (See Matthew 6:24.) On the other hand, you will not be afraid of man if you fear God!

REMOVING BARRIERS

Do you fear God, or have you become ensnared in the fear of man? As you draw near to God today in prayer, make a bold, new commitment to reject the fear of man and to give God an increased place of honor, glory and thanksgiving in your life. Doing so will increase your awareness of Him and will increase the fear of the Lord in your life.

PRAYER

Heavenly Father, I desire Your presence in my life. I long to learn more about how to fear You in every part of my life. I open my heart and ask You to fill my life with Your love and Your presence. I purpose to give You the place of honor You deserve with my actions and thoughts. Protect and shield me from the natural inclination to fear man whom I can see. Instead, give me a delight in fearing You—whom I can't see physically but love to serve and obey. I ask You to teach me the fear of the Lord, for it is the beginning of wisdom and the knowledge of You. Take me step by step along the path to Your presence. Amen.

 *Today's Light on the Path:*

LUKE 12

Hearts With Godly Fear

176

Oh, that they would always have hearts like this, that they might fear me and obey all my commands! If they did, they and their descendants would prosper forever.

—DEUTERONOMY 5:29

During the life of the early New Testament church, Ananias and his wife, Sapphira, brought an offering from a plot of land they sold. (See Acts 5:1–10.) They brought the offering and lied. (Many would have considered it just a "white lie.") They fell over dead because they lied about the amount of their offering in the presence of God's glory.

I used to wonder why people who have done the same in the presence of preachers today have not fallen over dead as well. The answer is because the presence of God was more powerful at the time of the Book of Acts than it is today. For example, Acts records that following this incident, Peter walked the streets of Jerusalem and the sick were healed as his shadow touched them. (See Acts 5:15.) We don't see such miracles today. Yet, as God's presence and glory increases, there will be similar accounts to the one in Acts 5.

Notice what happened after Ananias and Sapphira fell over dead: "Great fear gripped the entire church and all others who heard what had happened" (Acts 5:11). These believers realized they needed to rethink their treatment of God's presence and anointing. God says, "By those who come near Me I must be regarded as holy; and before all the people I must be glorified" (Lev. 10:3, NKJV).

God will withhold His glory to test and prepare us. Will we be reverent even when His presence is not manifest? In so many ways the modern church behaves like the children of Israel. When God parted the Red Sea, brought them across on dry ground and then drowned their enemies, they sang, danced and

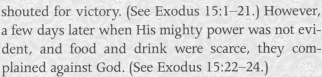

shouted for victory. (See Exodus 15:1–21.) However, a few days later when His mighty power was not evident, and food and drink were scarce, they complained against God. (See Exodus 15:22–24.)

Later Moses brought the people to Mount Sinai to consecrate them to God. God came down on the mountain in the sight of all His people. Moses then brought the people out of the camp to meet God. Exodus 20:18 says, "And when they saw the lightning and the smoke billowing from the mountain, they stood at a distance, trembling with fear." They pulled back in fear for their own lives, for they loved their own lives more than they loved God.

> And they said to Moses, "You tell us what God says, and we will listen. But don't let God speak directly to us. If he does, we will die!"
>
> "Don't be afraid," Moses said, "for God has come in this way to show you his awesome power. From now on, let your fear of him keep you from sinning!"
>
> —Exodus 20:19–20

Notice that the fear of God gives you power over sin. Proverbs 16:6 says, "Evil is avoided by fear of the LORD."

The account in Exodus continues, "As the people stood in the distance, Moses entered into the deep darkness where God was" (Exod. 20:21). The people drew back while Moses drew near. Moses feared God. Therefore, he was unafraid. However, the people did not fear God, and they were afraid.

The fear of God draws you toward God's presence, not away from it. But the fear of man causes you to withdraw from God and His glory.

When we are bound by the fear of man, we will feel more comfortable in the presence of men than in the presence of God, even in church! The reason: The presence of God lays open our hearts and brings conviction. (See Luke 12:2–5.) Oh, that we might fear God and not man. We then must obey His commands as we continue along the pathway into His presence.

REMOVING BARRIERS

Do you run toward God's presence, or do you often pull away? Ask God to reveal your heart and expose your motives for not pressing in more deeply to God's presence.

PRAYER

Lord, Scripture tells us that we are blessed because we believe in You without seeing You. As I study Your Word concerning the fear of the Lord, cause my faith to increase. I don't want just to say I fear You, but I desire to live it! I purpose to obey Your commandments and grow in my knowledge of You. I am grateful that the fear of the Lord empowers me to conquer sin. Through Your powerful grace I will lean on You and draw closer to Your presence. I commit into Your capable hands my every need during every hour of this day. In the name of Jesus, amen.

 *Today's Light on the Path:*

EXODUS 19–20

Section Eight

INTIMACY WITH GOD

Pathway to His Presence

When you are intimate with someone, he or she occupies a place in your heart— regardless of interruptions or challenges to your relationship. This is certainly true of our relationship with the eternal Father. No matter what comes against us or passes through our lives, He remains true to us. But what about our focus during times of trouble? The apostle James encourages us, "Dear brothers and sisters, whenever trouble comes your way, *let it be an opportunity for joy*. For when your faith is tested, your endurance has a chance to grow. So let it grow, for when your endurance is fully developed, you will be *strong in character and ready for anything*. If you need wisdom—if you want to know what God wants you to do—ask him, and he will gladly tell you. He will not resent your asking. But when you ask him, be sure that you really expect him to answer, for a doubtful mind is as unsettled as a wave of the sea that is driven and tossed by the wind" (James 1:2–6, emphasis added).

Notice that God says, "Let it be an opportunity for joy." He does not say, "Let it be part joy and part sorrow." There is not to be any mixture of sorrow in our hearts.

Now, it's easy to maintain joy when everything is going great. But God wants us to draw our strength from joy during times of trouble. Why does the Bible say this? Because God knows that "the joy of the LORD is your strength!" (Neh. 8:10). Joy is a spiritual force that gives us strength.

God promises "beauty for ashes, joy instead of

mourning, praise instead of despair" (Isa. 61:3). One day while I (John) was at home alone, I sensed a spirit of heaviness. I wanted to press in closer to God, so I picked up my Bible to read, but I could barely keep track of the words. I began to pray, and that was even more difficult. Inside I sensed the Spirit of God nudging me to turn on one of my praise tapes.

Frustrated, I went up to the loft where our stereo was and turned on some praise music. I sang along with it, and when the medley of songs was over, I played it a second time. This time, as I sang along, I began to hear what I was singing. Joy bubbled up into my soul, and I danced and sang around the loft. I noticed that my focus had shifted from myself to the greatness of God and the love of Jesus. I celebrated this revelation through dance and song for the next thirty minutes. When it was over, I realized all the heaviness had lifted. I felt life and strength flowing through me when thirty minutes earlier I had felt lifeless.

The prophet Isaiah says, "With joy you will drink deeply from the fountain of salvation!" (Isa. 12:3). As I praised Him my focus changed, and I exchanged my heaviness for the joy of the Lord. I had drawn strength from the fountain of salvation. Praise keeps our eyes on the joy set before us. In order to draw nearer, we must behold Him. These final five devotions examine this area of intimacy with God.

Intimacy isn't something that happens overnight. Intimacy is a function of growth and trust. It's a

183

process that often involves pain as well as pleasure. It is a time when we dare to be vulnerable enough to lay aside the masks and step out from behind the walls and be seen as we are. He loves us intimately and deeply. He will not reject our attempt to draw nearer. He invites us closer to see and be seen. Let's pray as we step onto this pathway to His presence.

The Wonder of God's Greatness

186

My soul thirsts for you; my whole body longs for you . . . I have . . . gazed upon your power and glory.

—Psalm 63:1–2

For us to give God the reverence that He deserves, we must pursue the knowledge of the greatness of His glory. This was the heart cry of Moses when he boldly pleaded, "Please let me see your glorious presence" (Exod. 33:18).

The more extensive our comprehension of God's greatness (though in itself it is incomprehensible), the greater our capacity for fear or reverence of Him. For this reason the psalmist encourages us, "For God is the King of all the earth; sing praises with understanding" (Ps. 47:7, NKJV). We are invited to behold His greatness. Yet we are also told by the psalmist, "Great is the Lord, and greatly to be praised; and His greatness is unsearchable" (Ps. 145:3, NKJV).

Isaiah had a vision of the unsearchable glory of God. He saw the Lord in His throne room, high and lifted up, and His glory filled the room. Around Him stood massive angels called seraphim, who, because of God's great glory, covered their faces with their wings and cried out, "Holy, holy, holy is the LORD Almighty! The whole earth is filled with his glory!" (Isa. 6:3).

Throughout the history of man, God's glory has repeatedly been reduced to our image and to the measure of corruptible man. This has been great folly. Even today we see this evidenced to an alarming degree in the church. Let's meditate for a moment on the wonder of His works, for His creation preaches quite a sermon and gives us points to ponder.

Psalm 145:10–11 says, "All of your works will thank you, LORD. . . . They will talk together about the glory of your kingdom; they will celebrate examples of your power."

I have four sons. There was a period of time when they were too interested in a certain professional basketball player. He is one of the most popular athletes in America and idolized by many in this nation. During an outing at the Atlantic coast, we had just come in from the beach where the boys had tumbled and danced in the waves. As we dried off after our swim, I sat down with my three oldest boys.

"Boys, that's a massive ocean out there, isn't it?"

In unison, they answered, "Yeah, Dad."

I continued, "You can only see about one or two miles of it, but the ocean actually goes on for thousands of miles. And this one isn't even the biggest ocean. There is another even bigger one called the Pacific Ocean. Then there are two more besides it."

The boys all nodded in silent wonder as they listened to the power of the pounding surf now at high tide outside our window.

Knowing that to some degree my sons had grasped my thought regarding the overwhelming amount of water, I asked, "Boys, do you know that God weighed all the water that you see, and all the oceans I have just described, in the palm of His hand?" (See Isaiah 40:12.)

Their mouths and eyes registered genuine amazement. They had been impressed because this famous sports figure could palm a basketball!

The Bible declares that God can measure the universe with the span of His hand (Isa. 45:12). Holding my own hand before them, I demonstrated that a span was the distance from the tip of my thumb to the tip of my pinkie. "God can measure the universe in the distance from His thumb to the tip of His smallest finger!" I then told them that God put the stars and our sun in orbit with His fingers. They were amazed. The basketball player's greatness was brought back to proper perspective.

In the pathway to His presence, we need to constantly consider God's greatness. Such awareness will deepen our understanding of God. Also we will continually praise God for His great love for us—even in light of His greatness.

REMOVING BARRIERS

As our understanding of God's greatness increases, our capacity to fear God and grow in our intimacy with Him increases as well. Visit a place in which the magnificence of God's creation reveals the awesome power of His character. Praise and thank Him aloud for the wonder you see. Ask Him to reveal Himself through the wonder of His handiwork.

PRAYER

God, Your greatness is unsearchable. I marvel at Your ability to measure the vast universe with Your hand. Increase my intimacy with You. I thirst for the knowledge of You and long to see Your power and glory. In Jesus' name, amen.

 *Today's Light on the Path:*

JOB 38–42

The Fear of God vs. Being Afraid of God

190

Then the Lord told Moses, "Go down and prepare the people for my visit. Purify them today and tomorrow, and have them wash their clothing. Be sure they are ready on the third day, for I will come down upon Mount Sinai as all the people watch."

—EXODUS 19:10–11

Israel had just left Egypt and was led by Moses to Mount Sinai, where God would reveal His glory. Moses spoke to the Israelites, but his words also speak to us. Before God manifested His glory, the people were to sanctify themselves.

> On the morning of the third day, there was a powerful thunder and lightning storm, and a dense cloud came down upon the mountain. There was a long, loud blast from a ram's horn, and all the people trembled. Moses led them out from the camp to meet with God, and they stood at the foot of the mountain. All Mount Sinai was covered with smoke because the LORD had descended on it in the form of fire. The smoke billowed into the sky like smoke from a furnace, and the whole mountain shook with a violent earthquake.
>
> —EXODUS 19:16–18

God manifested Himself not only by sight, but He also manifested Himself by voice and sound. When Moses spoke, God answered him in the hearing of all. Often today the Lord is referred to as our friend in the casual sense of almost being a buddy. If we could but glimpse what Moses and the children of Israel saw, we might have a significant change of view. He is the Lord, and He has not changed! Read carefully the reaction of the children of Israel when God came:

> When the people heard the thunder and the loud blast of the horn, and when they saw the lightning and the smoke billowing from the mountain, they stood at a distance, trembling with fear. And they

said to Moses, "You tell us what God says, and we will listen. But don't let God speak directly to us. If he does, we will die!"

—Exodus 20:18–19

Notice that the people trembled and drew back. They no longer wanted to hear God's audible voice. Neither did they want to look upon or be in the presence of His glory—they were unable to bear it.

"And Moses said to the people, 'Do not fear; for God has come to test you, and that His fear may be before you, so that you may not sin'" (Exod. 20:20, NKJV). This verse makes a distinction between being afraid of God and fearing Him. Moses feared God, but the people did not. It is an infallible truth that if we do not fear God, we will be afraid of Him at the revelation of His glory, for every knee shall bow to Him, if not out of godly fear then out of terror. (See 2 Corinthians 5:10–11.)

Look at the difference in the responses to God's manifested glory: Israel drew back, but Moses drew near. This illustrates the different responses of believers today. Like Moses, we need to fear God so that we may be able to draw toward God's holy presence.

The Beginning of Knowledge

194

Friendship with the Lord is reserved for those who fear him. With them he shares the secrets of his covenant.

—Psalm 25:14

Walking in intimate friendship with God is the heart's desire of every true believer. It is the only thing that will ever bring lasting fulfillment. It is God's motive for the Creation and His purpose in redemption. It is the very focus of His heart and a treasure reserved for those who fear Him.

Consider Solomon's wisdom: "Fear of the LORD is the beginning of knowledge" (Prov. 1:7). Is Solomon referring to scientific knowledge? No, for many scientists exalt man and have no fear of God. Does this verse refer to social or political accomplishment? No, for the world's ways are foolishness to God. Is it knowledge of the Scriptures? No, for although the Pharisees were experts in the law, they were displeasing to God. Our answer is found in Proverbs 2:4–5: "Search for them [God's words] as you would for lost money or hidden treasure. Then you will understand what it means to fear the LORD, and you will gain knowledge of God."

The fear of the Lord is the beginning, or starting place, of an intimate relationship with God. Intimacy is a two-way relationship. For example, I know about the president of the United States. I can list information about his accomplishments and his political stance, but I do not actually know him. I lack a personal relationship with him. Those in the president's immediate family and his close associates know him.

Another example would be those of us who are so taken with the professional athletes and Hollywood celebrities of our day. Their names are common in the households of America. The media has laid bare their personal lives through numerous television interviews and newspaper and magazine articles. I hear fans talk as though these celebrities were close friends. I have even seen people caught up emotionally in the marriage problems of their favorite celebrities and have watched them grieve as if they were family members when their screen heroes died.

If these fans ever met their celebrity hero on the street, they would not even receive a nod of acknowledgment. If they were bold enough to stop this celebrity as he walked along, they might find the real person to be quite different from the image he portrays. The relationship between celebrities and their fans is a one-way relationship.

I have grieved over this same behavior in the church. I listen to believers talk about God as though He were just a buddy, someone they hang out with. They casually tell how God has shown them this or that. They say how much they desire His presence and hunger for His anointing. Often those who are young in the Lord or not yet stable in their relationship with the Lord will feel uncomfortable and spiritually deficient around these "close friends" of God.

Within minutes you will usually hear these individuals contradict themselves. They will say something that clearly reveals that their relationship with God is not unlike that between a fan and his favorite celebrity. They prove to be boasting about a relationship that is just not there.

The Lord said we cannot even begin to know Him on intimate terms until we fear Him. In other words, an intimate relationship and friendship with God will not even begin until the fear of God is firmly planted in our hearts.

We can attend services, read our Bibles daily and attend every prayer meeting scheduled. But if we do not fear God, we are only climbing the rungs of a religious ladder. What's the difference between these religious rituals and suffering from the celebrity syndrome? On our pathway into His presence we need to develop a truly intimate relationship with God.

REMOVING BARRIERS

Have you fallen into the "celebrity syndrome" with Father God, treating Him as you would a fan or a buddy? Repent for your casual attitude toward God. Ask Him to give you a deep respect for His holiness.

PRAYER

Lord, give me the insight and ability to fear You and grow in knowledge and wisdom. I confess that at times I've been too flippant about my attitude with You. You are holy and awesome. You hold the universe in Your hands yet know my every thought.

I pray that as I have chosen to fear You, my love for You and others will increase. I want to be a witness to others of the love of Jesus. Shine through my life today in Jesus' name. Amen.

 *Today's Light on the Path*

PSALM 34 • PSALM 27

Love and a Consuming Fire

Since we are receiving a kingdom which cannot be shaken, let us have grace, by which we may serve God acceptably with reverence and godly fear. For our God is a consuming fire.

—Hebrews 12:28–29, NKJV

The connection between reverence and godly fear is significant. If the fear of God were limited to just reverence, the writer would not have separated the concept of godly fear from it. Also notice that the writer did not conclude with, "For our God is a God of love," but rather, "Our God is a consuming fire." This statement about God corresponds to the reason the children of Israel backed away from His presence. "If the Lord our God speaks to us again, we will certainly die and be consumed by this awesome fire" (Deut. 5:25). God has not changed! He is still holy and still a consuming fire!

Yes, He is love, but He is also a consuming fire. Our judgment is much more severe than Israel's when we don't listen to and obey the voice of God. The grace we are given under the New Testament is not for us to use to live as we please. Why didn't the Israelites heed His voice? They did not fear God.

In our churches we have emphasized God's love and have heard very little about the fear of God. Because we have not preached the whole counsel of God, our view of love has been warped.

The love we've preached is a weak love. It does not have the power to lead us into consecrated living. It has dampened our fire and left us lukewarm. We have become like spoiled children who do not reverence their father! If we do not grow in the fear of the Lord, we risk the danger of becoming familiar with God and treating as common the things He considers holy.

The apostle Paul wrote, "Work out your own salvation with fear and trembling" (Phil. 2:12, NKJV). Where is our fear and trembling? Have we forgotten

He is the just Judge? Have we forgotten His judgment? Read the following exhortation carefully.

> Do not be haughty, but fear. For if God did not spare the natural branches [Israel], He may not spare you either. Therefore consider the goodness and severity of God: on those who fell, severity; but toward you, goodness, if you continue in His goodness. Otherwise you also will be cut off.
> —ROMANS 11:20–22, NKJV

We have become experts in His goodness. However, it is not just His goodness we are to consider. We must understand the severity of God as well. His goodness draws us to His heart, and His severity keeps us from pride and all manner of sin. A person who only considers the goodness forsakes the fear that will keep him from pride and worldliness. Likewise, the person who only considers the severity of God is easily ensnared in legalism. It is both the love and the fear of God that keep us on the narrow path to life.

I hope you realize that I am purposefully emphasizing this fear of God that has been so neglected in our modern church. I dearly love God and take great joy in being His child and in the privilege of serving Him. I know that it is the goodness of God that leads us to repentance (Rom. 2:4). I also know it is the fear of God and His judgment that keeps us from sinning willfully.

200

REMOVING BARRIERS

Take some time and consider how God is both love and a consuming fire. Fire consumes the dross, and only pure gold is left. Let the fire of God's holy presence consume the sin and evil in your life and purify you for His holy service.

PRAYER

Heavenly Father, You are the all-consuming fire. I pray You will teach me how to love You more deeply and fear You with my whole heart. Lord, help me to follow the example of King David, who was a man after Your own heart. I realize that such depth in my relationship with you doesn't come from a single experience, but it occurs over months and years of consistently walking with You.

I long to be a person who has an intimate relationship with You. I purpose to fill my mind and heart with thoughts about You throughout my day. I want to grow more like Jesus day by day. In the powerful name of Jesus, amen.

 *Today's Light on the Path:*

ISAIAH 60

Pursue Godly Wisdom

My child, listen to me and treasure my instructions. Tune your ears to wisdom, and concentrate on understanding. Cry out for insight and understanding. Search for them as you would for lost money or hidden treasure. Then you will understand what it means to fear the Lord, and you will gain knowledge of God. For the Lord grants wisdom! From his mouth come knowledge and understanding.

—PROVERBS 2:1–6

Wisdom was so ingrained in Solomon that he knew what he wanted before God even asked him. He bore the heartfelt desire of his parents to know God's wisdom and to understand His holy fear. He knew of the brother who had come before him. He'd heard that the Lord loved him and had set him apart as a prince among princes. He knew that only wisdom could preserve and guide his life as king.

Solomon pursued wisdom all his life. As wise as he was, he disobeyed God's command to never marry a foreign wife. He married many of them, and they pulled his heart away from following the Lord, eventually causing him to stray from following God with his whole heart.

After a prosperous forty-year reign, Solomon looked back on his life and gave this summation of his entire search:

> Here is my final conclusion: Fear God and obey his commands, for this is the duty of every person. God will judge us for everything we do, including every secret thing, whether good or bad.
> —ECCLESIASTES 12:13–14

At the end of his life, he returns to the wisdom of his parents. He exhorts those who read his words to first fear God and secondly to keep God's commandments. Why? Because the day will come when each of us must stand before the greatest King and watch as He brings our every word and deed into judgment. Solomon was at the threshold of that judgment and could sense the urgency of what truly merited his time and attention.

As the wisest of all, he knew what was truly valuable. He perceived the scale of God's eternal and true measure. God is the ultimate Judge of the true measure of a person. He is only interested in what remains after the fire of truth purges all the chaff and dross.

The measure of faith causes us to believe that God is just and that He is good. Because of these two truths we can freely embrace the gospel and hide ourselves in Christ. This grants us His righteousness. We are to place no trust in ourselves or in our own righteousness. Denying ourselves, we are to embrace the cross.

The love of God draws us closer. As we behold Him, we are transformed by His image into His likeness.

The fear of God keeps us from returning to the path of destruction. It guards us and cleanses us from impurity. Holy fear imparts a saving knowledge of the Lord. It is the light that draws us nearer, while His love assures us and His faith empowers us.

These three strands—faith, love and holy fear—when woven and braided firmly together provide a safe and sure hold for us. They are the criteria by which God judges the motivations of our hearts. This standard is applied to all who embrace the cross.

It no longer matters how we are measured by this world or by the law, for a new and living way has been set before us. To enter deeper into His presence and embrace an intimate relationship with the eternal God, we must grow in our faith, love and holy fear. Yet we can't grow in our own power—we must cast ourselves into God's capable hands and use the power and strength of God's Spirit.

REMOVING BARRIERS

Set your heart to pursue God's wisdom. Memorize God's promises and guard your time spent reading the Bible. Listen to worship music throughout your day and cultivate a atmosphere for His presence. Write down verses from Proverbs that speak directly to your heart. Allow times of quiet meditation for the Holy Spirit to bring you into the place of the intimate knowledge of the Father.

PRAYER

God, I know it's impossible in my own power or energy to have an intimate relationship with You. Therefore I ask You, Holy Spirit, to continually lead me in love, faith and reverential fear of God. I don't want to stay the same as I walk into Your presence. I long to grow and become more like the Lord Jesus. Thank You for the Scriptures and the example of Jesus walking the earth. Awaken in me a desire to know You more, and then give me Your strength for the path ahead. Thank You for the blessing of growing intimate with You. I ask these things in the powerful name of Jesus Christ, amen.

 *Today's Light on the Path:*

PROVERBS 4

Other Books by
John and Lisa Bevere

THE FEAR OF THE LORD by John Bevere

 More than ever, there's something missing in our churches, our prayers and in our personal lives. It's what builds intimacy in our relationship with God. It's what makes our lives real and pure. It's what transforms us into truly Spirit-led children of God. It is the fear of the Lord.

This book exposes our need to fear God and challenges us to reverence God anew in our worship and daily lives. This profound message will provoke you to honor God in a way that will revolutionize your life.

THE BAIT OF SATAN by John Bevere

Your Response Determines Your Future

 This book exposes one of the most deceptive snares Satan uses to get believers out of the will of God. It is the trap of offense.

Most who are ensnared do not even realize it. But everyone must be made aware of this trap, because Jesus said, "It is impossible that offenses will not come" (Luke 17:1). The question is not, "Will you encounter the bait of Satan?" Rather it is, "How will you respond?" *Your response determines your future!* Don't let another person's sin or mistake affect your relationship with God!

"This book by my friend John Bevere is strong, strong, strong! I found new help from his fresh insights and uncompromising desire to help each of us recognize Satan's baits and avoid them at all costs."

—*Oral Roberts, Oral Roberts University*

BREAKING INTIMIDATION by John Bevere

How to Overcome Fear and Release the Gift of God in Your Life

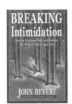

Countless Christians battle intimidation. Yet they wrestle with the side effects rather than the source. Intimidation is rooted in the fear of man. Proverbs 29:25 says, "The fear of man brings a snare . . ." This snare limits us so we don't reach our full potential.

Paul admonished Timothy, "The gift of God in you is dormant because you're intimidated!" (2 Tim. 1:6–7, paraphrased). An intimidated believer loses his position of spiritual authority. Without this authority his gifting from God remains dormant.

The Bible is filled with examples of God's people facing intimidation. Some overcame while others were overcome. This book is an in-depth look at these ancient references and present-day scenarios. The goal: to expose intimidation, break its fearful grip and release God's gift and dominion in your life.

This is an urgent message for every child of God who desires to reach their full potential in their walk with Christ. Don't allow fear to hold you back!

THE DEVIL'S DOOR by John Bevere

In *The Bait of Satan*, John Bevere exposed the devil's number-one trap for believers today. In *The Devil's Door*, he reveals the easiest way the enemy gains access in the lives of Christians—through rebellion. Satan cleverly deceives believers into thinking that submission is bondage and that rebellion is freedom. This revealing book exposes the devil's deception, blocks his entrance into your life, and helps you enjoy God's blessing and protection.

VICTORY IN THE WILDERNESS by John Bevere

God, Where Are You?

Is this the cry of your heart? Does it seem your spiritual progress in the Lord has come to a halt—or even regressed? You wonder if you have missed God or somehow displeased Him, but that is not the case . . . you've just arrived at the wilderness! Now, don't misunderstand the purpose of the wilderness. It is not God's rejection, but the season of His preparation in your life. God intends for you to have *Victory in the Wilderness*.

Understanding this season is crucial to the successful completion of your journey. It is the road traveled by patriarchs and prophets in preparation for a fresh move of God.

THE VOICE OF ONE CRYING by John Bevere

A Prophetic Message for Today!

God is restoring the prophetic to turn the hearts of His people to Him. Yet often this office is reduced to merely one who predicts the future by a word of knowledge or wisdom . . . rather than a declaration of the church's true condition and destiny. Many, fed up with hype and superficial ministry, are ready to receive the true prophetic message.

YOU ARE NOT WHAT YOU WEIGH by Lisa Bevere

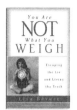

Are you tired of reading trendy diet books, taking faddish pills and ordering the latest in television infomercial exercise equipment? If you're like most women, what you're really tired of is the tyranny of dieting.

Break free from the destructive cycle of dieting and apprehend true freedom. Discover riveting truths from God's Word with the power to set you free. Trade your *self* consciousness for a deeper consciousness of God.

OUT OF CONTROL AND LOVING IT! by Lisa Bevere

Is your life a whirlwind of turmoil? Are you hating it? It is because you are in control! In this candid and honest book, Lisa challenges you to relinquish control of your life to God. Are you tired of pretending to be free only to remain captive? This book contains in-depth insight into how fear causes us to hold on when we should let go! Are you holding on? Abandon yourself to God's care!

THE TRUE MEASURE OF A WOMAN by Lisa Bevere

A woman often measures herself and her own worth according to the standards set by others around her. Her self-esteem rises and falls with the whims of popular opinion as she allows other people to control how she thinks about herself.

In her frank, yet gentle manner, Lisa exposes the subtle influences and blatant lies that hold many women captive. This is an interactive book designed with questions to help you unveil the truth of God's Word. These truths will displace any lies and also help you discover who you are in Christ. It is only then that you can stop comparing yourself to others and begin to see yourself as God loves you.

PLEASE CONTACT JOHN BEVERE MINISTRIES:
· To receive JBM's free newsletter, *The Messenger*
· To receive a **FREE** and COMPLETE COLOR CATALOG
· To inquire about inviting the ministry of
John and Lisa Bevere to your organization

JOHN BEVERE MINISTRIES
P. O. Box 2002
Apopka, FL 32704-2002
Tel: 407-889-9617
Fax: 407-889-2065
E-mail: jbm@johnbevere.org
Website: www.johnbevere.org

In Europe, please contact the ministry at:

JOHN BEVERE MINISTRIES INTERNATIONAL LTD.
P.O. Box 138
Lichfield
WE14 OYL
United Kingdom
Tel./Fax: 44-1543-483383
E-mail:jbeurope@johnbevere.org

The Messenger television program airs on The
Christian Channel Europe. Please check your local
listings for day and time.